COOK:30.2

CREATE DELICIOUS WHOLEFOOD PLANT-BASED
MEALS FROM SCRATCH IN JUST 30 MINUTES

Introduction

Cook:30 Philosophy

This cookbook is all about how I cook at home.

It uses the recipes from my Revive Cafes and Revive Cafe Cookbooks, and combines them to create a complete meal in just 30 minutes.

After running two successful vegetarian cafes for over 10 years I have learned how to prepare food quickly and inject a lot of flavour without adding costly or unhealthful ingredients.

I am not a nutritionist and do not get into the finer points of dietary philosophy (of which there is plenty debate). But believe in using simple, wholegrain plant based food in my own diet, at home, in my cookbooks and cafes.

This means lots of fresh fruit and vegetables. Whole grains like brown rice, oats, quinoa. Plant-based proteins like beans, nuts, lentils and tofu. And making it taste awesome with international flavours and plenty of herbs and spices. Simple.

I do not use meat, dairy, seafood. I do not use white sugar, white flour or other highly processed ingredients. I avoid preservatives where I can. And while they do have their place on occasions, I do not use processed meat substitutes.

My natural recipe selection, preparation shortcuts and rustic presentation style would be scorned in most high level fine dining restaurants and cooking schools. However in a home (and casual cafe setting) they are quick to make, healthful and look and taste awesome!

How Cook:30 was born

After meeting me and viewing my cookbooks in New Zealand, Brenda Walsh invited me as a guest cook on her 3ABN Today programme with her sisters in 2013. My wife Verity and I travelled to the US to film this and we had a lot of fun sharing some Revive meals on their programme.

About that time Shelley Quinn (Program Development Manager) was looking for a new cooking programme for the 3ABN channel. Shelley asked me to share with her my vision for a cooking programme.

I explained that I would love to do a programme that would portray the way I cook at home.

Rather than having pre-measured ingredients sitting nicely on the counter ready for use, there would be multi-tasking, taking ingredients from the fridge and shelves, throwing in "approximate" amounts, and having several pots on the stove at once.

Everything would be made from scratch and I would not use canned vegetarian meals or specialist products - just common healthy plant-based foods that are readily available everywhere in the world.

It would have a lot of close-up shots and be fast-paced just like a cafe or home kitchen.

While this type of programme would surely be more work, it would more accurately reflect my style of cooking and would help viewers get a realistic picture of how they can cook healthy wholefood plant-based meals at home.

I thought perhaps my vision for the programme may be too much of a departure from other 3ABN cooking shows, however Shelley loved the concept and we immediately agreed to produce the series together.

To make it even easier for people to adopt these new cooking skills, I decided it would be great to do a cookbook which is what you are now holding.

All of the photographs in this book were shot during the taping of the Cook:30 programmes.

My mission

It is my mission in life to share with people how to eat and cook healthy. If you choose to put healthy food in your mouth, you will have a healthier body, get sick less often, reduce your chances of getting lifestyle diseases, and most likely live a lot longer.

However over and above those reasons, the best part about eating and living healthy is that you will have so much energy and vitality, feel great, and be able to achieve your dreams in life!

So give it a go, it is worth making the change, and I hope in this book and TV series that you will see how simple it can be.

I would love to hear how you find these recipes and how they impact your life.

Jeremy Dixon
jeremy@revive.co.nz

Contents

Episode Overview (Series 2)

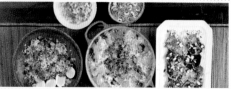

Revive Cafes

In 2003 my wife, Verity, and I treated ourselves to a 10 day cleanse at a health retreat. We had steam baths, massages, days of juice fasting, long walks, nutritional education, cooking classes, naturopathic consultations and 10 days of rest. We came back with a newfound vitality and zest for life.

By implementing simple changes in the ensuing months such as healthy eating, drinking plenty of water and exercise, we just felt so good!

However we realised on returning to Auckland that most cafes and eating places served food that was not really good for you.

I had a great career working for Sanitarium Health Food Company in Auckland for 10 years, as a marketer of healthy breakfast cereals like Weet-Bix. I had always had the dream of becoming a chef or owning a cafe, so in late 2004 I took a bold and risky move and decided to leave my great job to open a healthy cafe.

I quickly faced some hard realisations in researching successful food outlets. In order to be successful in hospitality it appeared that you needed to serve coffee, alcohol, soft drinks, sugary cakes, food full of white flour and be open long hours in the weekends. Against the advice of several people, I decided that I could not sleep at night serving people these kinds of food and beverages, and I continued on in search of a suitable location.

I purchased an existing cafe on Fort St and spent 2 months renovating, painting, organising and setting up my new cafe.

Thinking I knew it all from my Sanitarium career, I had to quickly learn the smarts of hospitality. It took a very stressful 12 months of menu amending, roster changing, marketing and staff training. However, I stuck at it, and eventually managed to get our formula working right.

We had queues out the door most lunchtimes and it made me very happy to know that so many people desired to eat heathy. It was a very intense 12 months, but the biggest thing I learned from this was to keep trying new things and to stick at it.

The cafe was so successful we opened a second Revive Cafe on Lorne St in 2008, just one kilometer uptown from the first cafe. In 2013 the lease ran out on the Fort St cafe so we moved a block away to a location twice the size in Wyndham St, where we now also have our central kitchen.

Revive has a salad bar with the options changing weekly. We serve a meal of the day, hotpot of the day and dahl of the day. We also serve a frittata of the week and soup of the week and some delicious healthy sweets and smoothies.

I have a passion for sharing health principles with people. So many people are dragging themselves through life content with being overweight, having headaches, health issues and feeling tired all the time.

I put a lot of time into the Revive weekly e-mails which include health tips and recipes. I also do cooking demonstrations where I share how simple it is to make healthy food, and have produced a series of cookbooks which are another way to share the recipes we use at Revive and to help people learn how to prepare healthy meals themselves.

I hope to see you at Revive sometime!

The 8 Keys to Healthy Living

These are the health principles that Revive Cafe and my life are founded on.

It is not enough to just eat healthy food in order to have complete energy and vitality. There are other simple things that create good health, and they are summarised by these 8 keys. They are easy to remember, they spell "NEWSTART".

The good news is that if you apply these simple 8 steps in your day-to-day living, you will notice dramatic improvements in your vitality, health and quality of life.

If you do not have great health and do not wake up each morning full of energy, chances are that you are not following some of these principles. Go through this list and start to implement one extra principle a week.

However, don't stop there, sign up for the regular Revive emails at www.revive.co.nz for weekly inspirational ideas and encouragement.

Disclaimer

Please note that these are general lifestyle principles only and it is recommended that you see a health professional regarding any serious health issues.

Fuel your body with quality food and feel great!

Good nutrition is all about putting fresh, quality, alive foods into your body. Make sure a large proportion (ideally 50-70%) of your diet is fresh, raw fruit and vegetables.

All good things in moderation and set yourself free from harmful things!

We all know that drugs, cigarettes, caffeine and alcohol are bad for our health and will shorten out lives. Our bodies are much better off if we avoid them altogether!

Feel alive with 30 minutes of exercise per day!

Keeping active is a key requirement for good health. Your body needs at least 30 minutes of exercise three times per week.

Increase your vitality with 8 glasses of water a day!

Most people need 8 glasses (2 litres/2 quarts) of pure water a day. Tea, coffee, juice, flavoured waters do not count! However a non-caffeinated herbal tea can be an occasional substitute.

Enjoy the rejuvenating benefits of sunshine!

The sun has many healing and rejuvenating properties. You feel so good when you get some sunshine.

Experts believe we need at least 10 minutes of sun on the inside of our arms as a minimum per day!

Breathe deeply to de-stress!

Breathe deeply and slowly. Many people are fast shallow breathers which does not allow your blood to get good oxygen.

Deep breathing will also help to relax you when you are stressed.

Sleep deeply with 8 hours of rest per night!

Most people generally need 8 hours sleep per night. If you are not waking feeling refreshed and rested you need to get to bed earlier.

Live in peace with a life full of great relationships!

This is all about the mental and spiritual side of health.

Seek God and enjoy all the blessings He has prepared for your life.

Cookbook Notes

Please read these notes before you start cooking as the recipes will make more sense.

Meals can be prepared using all the meal components in an episode, or you can pick and choose dishes from various episodes.

....

Recipe Preparation

The recipe timing page (at the beginning of each chapter) details the dishes to be prepared, the items and preparation required in your kitchen, and the approximate timings for each part.

Note: Due to other programme components, the "kitchen time" in the Cook:30 programme is recorded in 25 minutes, so the times on the video and in the cookbook will not line up exactly.

Making meals quickly does not happen by accident. Spending 5 minutes getting prepared before starting will save you many more minutes later and make the experience more enjoyable.

Read the recipe ingredients and method completely before beginning. Start with a clear and clean workspace and make sure you have assembled all items you require.

Complicated recipes (usually the main savoury dish) have been divided into different steps. Other simpler recipes generally have all their method and ingredients together.

....

Ingredient Notes

Coconut Milk, Coconut Cream, Cashew Cream

These are used to add creaminess to hot meals.

You can use coconut cream, coconut milk and cashew cream interchangeably. Coconut milk is runnier than coconut cream.

Garlic

I use garlic pressed through a garlic press. Alternatively you can finely chop peeled garlic.

I do not recommend using pre-prepared garlic purees as these just taste awful. Only use fresh garlic.

Ginger/Chilli/Lemongrass Puree

I often use ginger/chilli/lemongrass puree as it adds delicious flavour and is quick to use.

It is available from most supermarkets in tubes or tubs . Alternatively you can make your own by blending ginger/chilli/lemongrass with a little oil and storing in the refrigerator. Or you can peel and finely chop as you go.

Lemon & Lime Juice

Use freshly squeezed. Every lime and lemon varies in the amount of juice it yields so I have included measurements in tablespoons. A rough guide is 2 tablespoons of juice from a small lemon or lime.

Sweeteners/Honey/Date Puree

The recipes do not use added refined sugar. The most convenient natural sweetener is liquid honey which I have used in all recipes requiring sweetening.

Alternatively make up a batch of date puree which is an excellent and inexpensive sweetener.

To make date puree, simply blend equal amounts of dates and water into a smooth puree. This will keep in your refrigerator for a couple of weeks.

There are also other healthy sweeteners available such as apple sauce, agave and maple syrup.

Nuts

All nuts are shelled and raw unless stated.

Cashew nuts are a great creamy nut to use and relatively inexpensive. Cashew pieces (rather than whole) can be used in most dishes and are often half the price.

Oils

Use your favourite oil wherever "oil" is mentioned in the recipes. The oils I use the most are olive, grapeseed, coconut and rice bran oil.

Beans, Lentils & Chickpeas

I have used canned beans/chickpeas (garbanzo beans) as this is the most convenient for fast cooking. Drain cans before using.

If you can use freshly cooked beans they will taste better and are significantly cheaper. A 14oz (400g) can of beans is around 2 cups.

I recommend that you soak and cook your own beans and store them in your freezer. You will need to soak overnight in plenty of water. Then cook in fresh water until soft, which will be between

30 minutes and 2 hours, depending on the variety and age. Then freeze them in small containers.

To use, simply defrost by running some hot water over them in a sieve or colander for 30 seconds.

Thickeners: Arrowroot & Cornstarch

I use arrowroot and cornstarch (cornflour) for thickening sauces and desserts in the recipes in this book. Both are interchangeable however you may need to use more when using cornstarch and it may develop a more whiter colour.

Cooking Grains

For grains like brown rice and quinoa, I recommend you cook extra and store in your refrigerator for an easy ingredient to use in the following few days.

When cooking grains start with boiling water to save time, and return to the boil before turning down to a simmer (just bubbling). Do not stir while cooking and keep the lid on.

Onions

Brown onions are used when not specified however red or white onions can be used instead for most dishes. The onions I generally use for the recipes yield around 1½ cups when chopped.

General

Cooking Terms

Saute: to cook food on a high heat and in a little oil while stirring with a wooden spoon.
Simmer: to have food cooking at a low heat setting so it is just bubbling.
Roast: to bake in the oven covered with a little oil. Use fan bake setting to achieve more even cooking.

Mixing

To save dishes, you can mix most recipes in the pot or pan you are cooking in or for salads in your serving bowl.

With salads, mix with your hands if possible. Gently lift up the ingredients and let them fall down with gravity rather than squeezing.

Taste Test

It is difficult to get a recipe that works 100% the same every time, especially when you are using fresh and natural ingredients. Vegetable sizes vary, spices and herbs differ in strength and you can even get differences in evaporation rates with different sized pots.

Make sure you taste test every dish before you serve and be willing to add more seasoning or a little more cooking time if necessary.

Peeling Vegetables

If in good clean condition, I do not peel potatoes, carrots or sweet potato (kumara). You gain extra vitamins, higher yield and save a lot of time.

Quantities

The yield and servings for each dish are an estimate and will vary depending on cooking times and ingredient size.

I have used one cup as an average serving size.

The combined meals in general will feed 4–6 people however this will vary greatly so you will need to determine this.

I usually plan to over cater. I can then fill my fridge with leftovers to last me 1–2 days, or send guests home with lunch for the next day!

Gluten Free & Dairy Free

A large proportion of the recipes are gluten free and all are meat, egg and dairy free. If you have any allergies you will need to check whether each recipe is suitable and make adjustments as required.

Kitchen tools

Pots/Pans

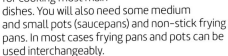

I recommend a large non-stick frying pan or cast iron pan to be used for cooking most main dishes. You will also need some medium and small pots (saucepans) and non-stick frying pans. In most cases frying pans and pots can be used interchangeably.

Blenders/Food Processors

Some recipes require a food processor (usually with an S blade). This is generally for non-liquid items.

Smoothies, dressings and pourable recipes require a blender or liquidiser (usually a tall jug with 4 pronged blades). In most cases a stick blender can be used.

Knives

You will need a good sharp knife to make preparation fast, safe and accurate.

Many people end up with 10 cheap $20 knives in their drawer. I recommend just buying 1 good quality (up to $200) chefs knife that will last your lifetime and make your cooking experience more enjoyable.

Jacket potatoes are great! Here are my favourite toppings.

Nutty Seedy Slaw

Creamy Thyme Mushrooms

Tuscan Lentil & Tomato Stew

Jacket Potatoes

Mango Chia Glass

Get ready before you start

Jug	Oven	Counter	Ready on stovetop	Plugged in and ready	Preparation required
Boiling with 2 cups of water	Fan bake 400°F (200°C) Oven tray	Chopping board Sharp chefs knife Serving dishes and glasses	Medium frying pan Large pot	Blender or stick blender	Prepare & start to bake potatoes 30 minutes ahead of time

Timing

:00	DESSERT	Blend honey, cashews, mango, water, add chia and refrigerate.
:04	LENTILS	Saute onion, celery.
:08	MUSHROOMS	Saute onions, mushrooms, garlic.
:11	LENTILS	Add lentils, tomatoes, honey, tomato paste.
:16	SEEDY SLAW	Slice vegetables and make dressing.
:21	MUSHROOMS	Make and add cashew cream, plate up with chopped thyme.
:24	DESSERT	Pour mango chia pudding into dessert glasses.
:27	VEGES	Dice veges and plate up with greens and side serving of hummus.
:30	FINISH	Cut potatoes. Serve alongside mushrooms, veges, lentils, coleslaw.

Nutty Seedy Slaw

Coleslaw is awesome on top of baked potatoes!
MAKES 4 X 1 CUP SERVES

1 cup red cabbage

1 cup white cabbage

1 cup carrot

2 cups baby spinach

½ cup mung bean sprouts

1 tablespoon fennel seeds

2 tablespoons mixed nuts and seeds such as cashew nuts, pumpkin seeds, sesame seeds, sunflower seeds

¼ cup mixed flat leaf parsley and mint

¼ cup Easy Tahini Dressing

Slice cabbage thinly and add to a serving bowl.

Grate carrot and add to bowl.

Add baby spinach and mung bean sprouts.

Pour dressing over the vegetables and mix together gently with your hands.

Add chopped Italian parsley and torn mint leaves.

Sprinkle chopped cashew nuts, fennel, pumpkin, sunflower and sesame seeds over the top for crunchiness.

Tip: If making coleslaw for a lot of people, save time by using your food processor and it's attachments.

Easy Tahini Dressing

An easy dressing you can use on almost anything.
MAKES ¼ CUP

1 tablespoon liquid honey

2 tablespoons lemon juice (around 1 lemon)

2 tablespoons tahini

¼ teaspoon salt

Add all ingredients to a small bowl and stir with a spoon until smooth and well combined.

Creamy Thyme Mushrooms

MAKES 3 X 1 CUP SERVES

7oz (200g) mushrooms (flat and button and others)

1 onion diced

2 cloves garlic crushed

1 tablespoon oil

½ cup water

½ cup cashew nuts raw

¼ teaspoon salt

optional: 2 tablespoons soy sauce

garnish: 2 tablespoons fresh thyme

Saute mushrooms, onion, garlic, oil until soft.

Blend cashews and water together to make cream. Add with salt and optional soy sauce to mushroom dish.

Warm through, then pour into serving dish.

Garnish with finely chopped thyme – it goes really well with mushrooms so make sure you do not miss adding the garnish!

Tuscan Lentil & Tomato Stew

MAKES 4 X 1 CUP SERVES

1 onion finely chopped
1 tablespoon oil
1 cup celery diced
2 cloves garlic crushed
½ cup red lentils
2 cups boiling water
12oz can (400g) tomatoes crushed
2 tablespoons liquid honey
2 tablespoons tomato paste
2 tablespoons lemon juice
½ teaspoon salt
1 tablespoon mixed herbs
garnish: cilantro (fresh coriander)

In a pot or pan saute the onion, oil, celery and garlic for 5 minutes or until soft.

Add lentils, water, tomatoes, honey and tomato paste.

Turn up to heat, when it starts to boil turn heat down and simmer for 15 minutes.

Add lemon juice, salt and mixed herbs.

Garnish with chopped cilantro.

Jacket Potatoes

SERVES 4

....

4 large potatoes, skin on
oil spray
toppings

Lightly spray potatoes with oil. Put on oven tray and bake at 400°F (200°C) for 45 minutes or until cooked through.

Make a cut across the top of the potatoes lengthwise, then widthwise, and use your fingers to squeeze them open by pushing all 4 corners up and into the middle of the potato.

Top with Salad Vegetables, hummus, Creamy Thyme Mushrooms and Tuscan Lentil & Tomato stew.

Tip: If your oven has a timer, set the oven so the potatoes are ready when you get home.

Salad Vegetables

MAKES 4 X 1 CUP SERVES

2 cups tomato (mixed colours) diced
1 telegraph cucumber
2 cups mixed green leaves (such as baby spinach, green beet tops, baby lettuce leaves)

Dice tomatoes and cucumber and plate up with mixed baby green leaves.

Mango Chia Glass

Chia seeds swell up to make a lovely creamy dessert.
SERVES 4

2 tablespoons liquid honey

¼ cup cashew nuts raw

1 ¼ cups water

2 cups frozen mango (slightly defrosted)

¼ cup chia seeds

garnish: cashew cream (¼ cup cashews and ¼ cup water, blended together)

garnish: blueberries

garnish: mint leaves

Add honey, cashews, water and mango to a blender and blend untl smooth. Add more water to blender if needed to make it process smoothly.

Add chia seeds and stir through with a spoon (do not blend).

Pour mango chia pudding into dessert glasses. Refrigerate 30 minutes and allow the chia seeds to swell and thicken the dessert.

Garnish with squiggle of cashew cream, fresh blueberries and mint leaves.

Tip: If the mango is particularly sweet you may not need to add honey.

Tip: There can be great variation in how well chia seeds swell. Chia seeds that have been heat treated don't swell quite so well.

All my favourite
ingredients in one
Mega Stir Fry!

Mega Stir Fry

Raspberry & Mint Smoothie

Get ready before you start

Jug	Oven	Counter	Ready on stovetop	Plugged in and ready	Preparation required
Boiling with 2 cups of water	Fan bake 350°F (180°C) Oven tray	Chopping board Sharp chefs knife Serving dishes and glasses	Large pot Medium pot Large frying pan Small frying pan	Blender or stick blender	

Timing

:00	VEGES	Put rice on to boil.
:01	POTATOES	Chop and place in oven.
:05	VEGES	Saute onion mix. Fry tempeh separately.
:11	AIOLI	Blend all ingredients.
:17	VEGES	Add broccoli, cauliflower, salt.
:19	NUTS	Add cashews, almonds, pecans and sunflower seeds to hot pan.
:21	VEGES	Add rice to main pan and stir.
:23	SMOOTHIE	Blend all ingredients and pour into glasses.
:27	NUTS/VEGES	Nuts: Add sesame seeds. Add tamari to tempeh and nuts and toss.
:30	FINISH	Layer rice, potato, tempeh, herbs, nuts and drizzle with ailoi.

Mega Stir Fry

This stir fry combines all my favourite ingredients into one yummy dish.
MAKES 7 X 1 CUP SERVES

Step 1 – Cook Rice

1 cup brown rice long grain

2 cups boiling water

Put rice and boiling water in a small pot and bring to boil. Turn down to low heat. Place the lid on, do not stir. Let simmer for 20 minutes or until cooked.

Step 2 – Saute Onion Mix

1 cup onion diced roughly

1 cup celery (approx. 2 medium stalks) diced small

1 cup carrots sliced

1 fennel bulb and stalks sliced

2 cloves garlic crushed

2 tablespoons ginger puree

1 tablespoon oil

In a large pan saute onion, celery, carrots, fennel, garlic, ginger and oil for 5 minutes or until soft.

Step 3 – Saute Tempeh

8oz (230g) pack tempeh
½ tablespoon coconut or other oi

In a small pan, saute cubed tempeh and oil.

Step 4 – Finish

1 cup broccoli florets small

1 cup cauliflower florets small

¼ teaspoon salt

1 tablespoon tamari

Roasted Sweet Potato

Tamari Toasted Nuts & Seeds

garnish: cilantro (fresh coriander)

garnish: mint

garnish: Cashew & Lime Aioli

Cut broccoli and cauliflower into florets and add with salt to pan.

Add rice to large pan and stir through – note you want about $2/3$ of the pan to be vegetables.

Add tamari to tempeh and toss briefly.

Serve rice in large bowl and top with tempeh, Roasted Sweet Potato, Tamari Toasted Nuts & Seeds, fresh chopped cilantro and mint, and drizzle with Cashew & Lime Aioli.

Tamari Toasted Nuts & Seeds

MAKES 1 CUP

¼ cup sunflower seeds

¼ cup cashew nuts raw

¼ cup sliced almonds

¼ cup pecans

¼ cup sesame seeds

2 tablespoons tamari

Add cashews, almonds, pecans and sunflower seeds to a hot pan.

Toast for approximately 3 minutes.

Add sesame seeds near the end to toast lightly.

Add tamari to the nuts and toss.

Roasted Sweet Potato

MAKES 3 X 1 CUP SERVES

3 cups red sweet potato (kumara)
1 tablespoon oil
¼ teaspoon salt

Pre-heat oven to 350°F (180°C).

Dice unpeeled sweet potato and coat with oil and salt.

Place on parchment (baking) paper on a tray and roast in the oven for 20 minutes.

Raspberry & Mint Smoothie

SERVES 4

1 cup milk of your choice (soy, almond, rice or oat)

2 cups frozen raspberries

½ cup fresh mint

2 tablespoons liquid honey

2 medium ripe bananas

Put all ingredients into a blender and blend.

Tip: Raspberries are one of the more tart berries and work best with added sweetness.

Cashew & Lime Aioli

MAKES 1 CUP

1 ½ cups cashew nuts raw

1 clove garlic

2 teaspoons ground coriander

1 tablespoon seeded mustard

4 tablespoons lime juice (around 2 limes)

½ cup water

¼ teaspoon salt

optional: 1 teaspoon sweet chilli sauce or chilli paste

Place all ingredients into blender and blend until smooth and creamy.

Add more water if needed to achieve smooth blending consistency.

Dahls are so quick to make and delicious. Once you know how, it will become one of your favourites!

Tarka Dahl

Cucumber & Dill Salad

Seedy Sprinkle

Lemony Herb Rice

Cambodian Banana Fritters

Get ready before you start

Jug	Oven	Counter	Ready on stovetop	Plugged in and ready	Preparation required
Boiling with 5 ½ cups of water		Chopping board Sharp chefs knife Serving dishes and glasses	Large pan Medium pot Medium frying pan Small frying pan		

Timing

:00	RICE	Put on stove to boil.
:01	DAHL	Saute onion, garlic, ginger, oil.
:04	SALAD	Assemble all ingredients.
:10	DAHL	Add spices, lentils and water.
:11	FRITTERS	Mix up batter and start to fry; check periodically.
:17	SEEDS	Add seeds to hot pan and toast.
:20	DAHL	Add chickpeas, coconut milk, salt, honey, peas and heat through.
:26	RICE	Combine all ingredients in serving dish.
:30	FINISH	Plate up all dishes, serve and enjoy!

Tarka Dahl

MAKES 5 X 1 CUP SERVES

....

Step 1 – Onion Mix

1 onion finely chopped

3 cloves garlic crushed

2 tablespoons ginger puree

2 teaspoons oil

In a large pan saute the onion, garlic, ginger and oil for 5 minutes or until soft.

....

Step 2 – Add spices

2 teaspoons ground turmeric

2 teaspoons ground cumin

2 teaspoons ground coriander

Mix in the turmeric, cumin and coriander and stir briefly.

....

Step 3 – Cook Lentils

1 cup dried yellow lentils (toor dahl)

3½ cups boiling water

Add the lentils and water. Stir and simmer for 15 minutes or until lentils are soft. You can add more water if it dries out before it is cooked.

....

Step 4 – Finish and serve

12oz (400g) can chickpeas (garbanzo beans) drained

7oz (200ml) coconut milk

½ teaspoon salt

1 tablespoon liquid honey

1 cup frozen peas

garnish: coconut milk

garnish: sweet chilli sauce drizzled

garnish: cilantro (fresh coriander)

Stir in chickpeas, coconut milk, salt, honey and peas. Heat through and serve drizzled with coconut milk, sweet chilli sauce and fresh chopped cilantro.

....

Cucumber & Dill Salad

MAKES 3 X 1 CUP SERVES

1 telegraph cucumber diced

2 tablespoons dill chopped

½ teaspoon salt

2 tablespoons lemon juice (around 1 lemon)

½ cup soy or coconut yoghurt

Dice cucumber and add to medium serving bowl.

Chop dill finely and add together with salt, lemon juice and yoghurt.

Stir through and let sit, allowing flavours to mingle.

Seedy Sprinkle

This lovely crunchy topping adds great texture to any sacoury dish! Just serve in a small dish on the table.
MAKES 1 CUP

¼ cup pumpkin seeds

¼ cup sesame seeds

¼ cup sunflower seeds

¼ cup almond slices

¼ cup cashew pieces

1 tablespoon fennel seeds

Add nuts and seeds to hot pan and heat until lightly toasted.

Lemony Herb Rice

A great way to subtly flavour rice.
MAKES 3 x 1 CUP SERVES

1 cup brown rice long grain

2 cups boiling water

zest of 1 lemon

1 tablespoon cilantro (fresh coriander) chopped

1 tablespoon Italian parsley chopped

1 tablespoon mint chopped

¼ teaspoon salt

Put brown rice and just boiled water in a medium pot and bring back to boil.

Turn down to a simmer and cook using the absorption method – place the lid on, do not stir, and let simmer for 20 minutes.

Add lemon zest, cilantro, mint and Italian parsley.

Cambodian Banana Fritters

MAKES 12 FRITTERS

1 cup chickpea (besan) flour

1 cup water

3 ripe bananas

¼ cup slivered almonds

zest of 1 lemon

¼ teaspoon salt

1 tablespoon liquid honey

oil for frying

garnish: slivered almonds

garnish: liquid honey

Start with a medium mixing bowl and add chickpea flour.

Add ½ the water and stir until there are no lumps. Slowly add the remaining water until it's a nice consistent paste.

Roughly mash the bananas and add to mixing bowl. Add slivered almonds, lemon zest, salt and honey.

Heat a little oil in a non-stick fry pan and cook fritters for around 2 minutes each side or until golden brown and cooked right through.

Garnish with slivered almonds and honey drizzled on top.

Tip: You can substitute wholemeal flour for chickpea flour in this recipe.

Some classic
Italian favourites
of mine.

Chunky Italian Tomato Pasta

Italian Chickpea Salad

Leafy Green Salad

Pear & Apple Crumble

Get ready before you start

Jug	Oven	Counter	Ready on stovetop	Plugged in and ready	Preparation required
Boiling with 5 cups of water	Fan bake 350°F (180°C)	Chopping board Sharp chefs knife Serving dishes and glasses	Large pan Medium pot		

Timing

:00	PASTA	Put onion, garlic, herbs and oil on to saute.
:04	CRUMBLE	Assemble crumble and place in oven.
:10	PASTA	Put pasta in boiling water. Add tomatoes, honey, tomato paste.
:16	CHICKPEAS	Assemble all salad ingredients and dressing.
:22	GREEN SALAD	Assemble all ingredients on serving dish.
:28	PASTA	Drain pasta and add garnishes.
:30	FINISH	Serve and enjoy!

Chunky Italian Tomato Pasta

MAKES 6 X 1 CUP SERVES

Step 1 – Start Pasta

boiling water
7oz (200g) wholegrain spiral pasta
garnish: olive oil
garnish: ¼ teaspoon salt

Cook the pasta in boiling water for 8 minutes until firm to the bite or according to packet directions.   Drain immediately.

Drizzle with a tiny amount of olive oil and salt.

Step 2 – Saute Onion

1½ cups red onion largely diced (around 1 large onion)
6 cloves garlic crushed
1 teaspoon mixed herbs
1 tablespoon oil

In a pot or pan saute the onion, garlic, herbs and oil for 5 minutes or until the onion is soft.

Step 3 – Mix in Tomatoes

1 tablespoon liquid honey
2 x 12oz (400g) cans tomatoes crushed
4 tablespoons tomato paste
½ teaspoon salt

Add honey, tomatoes, tomato paste and salt to onion mix and warm through.

Step 4 – Serve & Garnish

½ cup basil chopped
½ cup Italian parsley chopped

Taste test before serving and add a little more salt and/or honey to taste. Serve with fresh chopped basil and Italian parsley on top.

Italian Chickpea Salad

Just add some olives and sundried tomatoes to transform chickpeas!
MAKES 4 X 1 CUP SERVES

....

2 x 12oz (400g) cans of chickpeas
(garbanzo beans)
½ green bell pepper (capsicum)
½ red bell pepper (capsicum)
8 sundried tomatoes
½ cup kalamata olives pitted
¼ cup Italian dressing
garnish: Italian parsley

Drain chickpeas and add to serving dish.

Add diced bell peppers, sliced sundried tomatoes and olives to serving dish.

Pour dressing over salad. Mix all ingredients together with your hands.

Serve garnished with parsley.

Tip: This salad is great stuffed inside fresh wholemeal pita bread with lettuce and avocado.

Italian Dressing

Simple and quick!
MAKES ¼ CUP

....

1 tablespoon liquid honey
½ teaspoon salt
1 tablespoon lemon juice
1 tablespoon olive oil

Add all dressing ingredients to a small bowl and stir to combine.

Leafy Green Salad

MAKES 3 X 1 CUP SERVES

8 stalks asparagus

1 red bell pepper (capsicum)

1 large carrot

1 telegraph cucumber (2 cups)

1 avocado

5oz (150g) leafy green salad mix

1 tablespoon lemon juice (around ½ lemon)

Break woody ends off asparagus stalks.

Thinly slice bell pepper lengthwise.

Peel skin off carrot and use the peeler to create ribbons of carrot.

Cut cucumber diagonally into half moons.

Dice avocado.

Scatter all ingredients onto serving plate.

Mix everything together and squeeze lemon juice over top.

Pear & Apple Crumble

You will not believe how quick this is!
SERVES 4

1 can apple sauce

1 can sliced pears

½ teaspoon cinnamon

¼ teaspoon nutmeg

3 cups granola/muesli

Pour apple sauce and canned pears into baking dish.

Slice pears with a knife if the chunks are larger than bite size.

Sprinkle cinnamon and nutmeg on top.

Pour granola/muesli over the fruit mixture. Place in oven and bake at 350°F (180°C) for 15 minutes.

Serve with fresh berries.

Tip: Make sure you use a healthy granola/muesli!

Episode
31

Supercharged Savoury Breakfast Bowl. A different way to enjoy a cooked breakfast – give it a go!

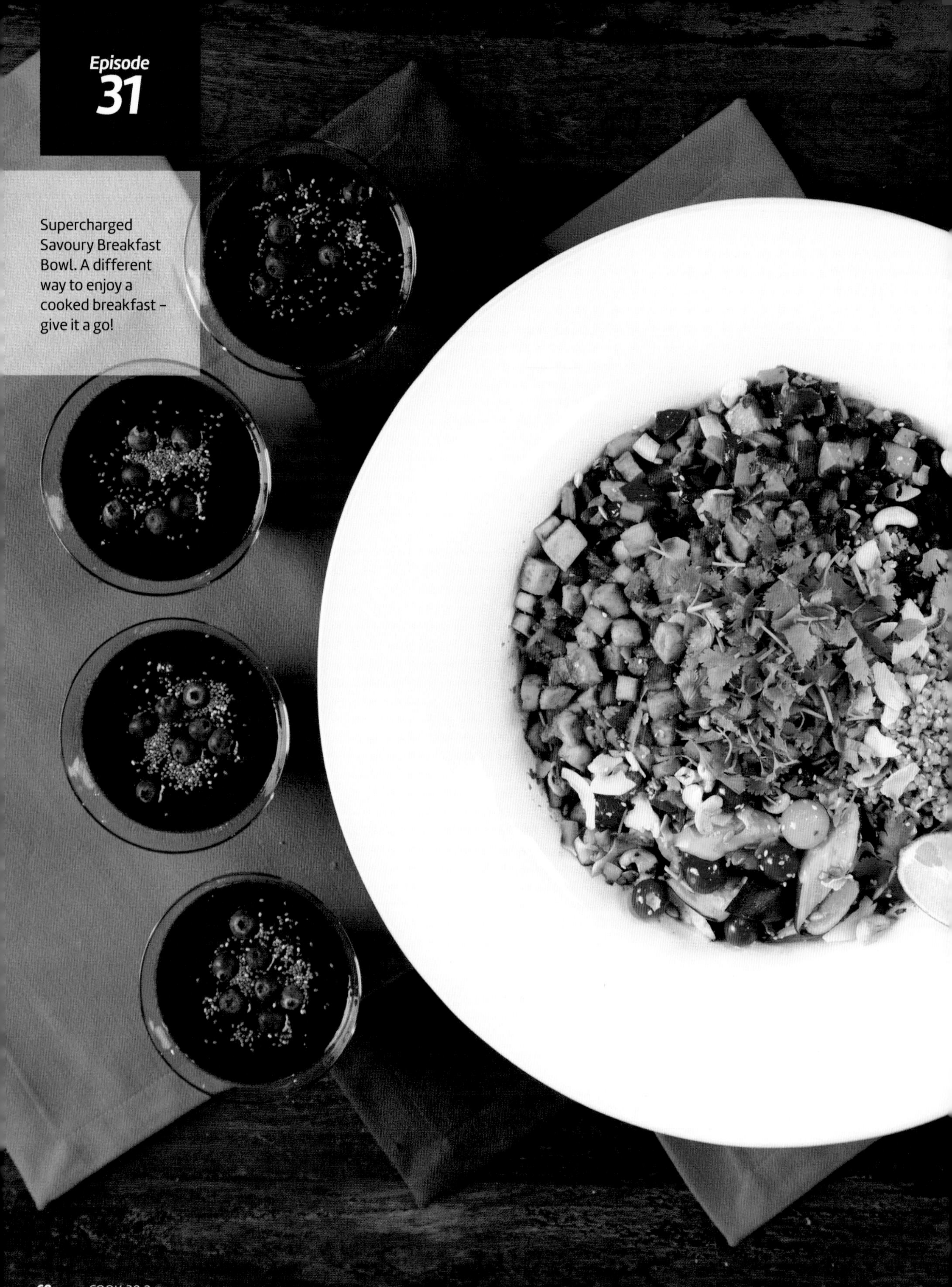

**Supercharged
Savoury
Breakfast Bowl**

**Blueberry
Power Shake**

Get ready before you start

Jug	Oven	Counter	Ready on stovetop	Plugged in and ready	Preparation required
	Fan bake 350°F (180°C)	Chopping board	2 medium frying pans	Blender or stick blender	
	Oven tray	Sharp chefs knife	1 small frying pan		
		Serving dish and glasses	Small pot		

Timing

:00	POTATOES	Chop sweet potato, bell pepper and onion and place in oven.
:05	BUCKW/TOFU	Add tofu ingredients to hot pan. Cook buckwheat in small pot.
:10	VEGES	Add zucchini, oil, garlic to hot pan.
:15	BUCKW/NUTS	Remove buckwheat from heat. Add nuts and seeds to hot pan.
:19	TOFU/VEGES	Remove tofu from heat/toss veges.
:21	BEANS	Add black beans and tamari sauce to pan and heat through.
:22	VEGES	Toss and turn off heat.
:24	NUTS	Add coconut to nut pan and toss.
:26	DESSERT	Blend all ingredients, pour into serving glasses and garnish.
:30	FINISH	Serve and enjoy!

Supercharged Savoury Breakfast Bowl

MAKES 4 X 1 CUP SERVES

Step 1 – Sweet Potato O'Brien

3 cups red sweet potato (kumara) diced (around 3 medium)

1 cup red bell pepper (capsicum) chopped (around 1 bell pepper)

1 cup red onion finely chopped (around 1 small onion)

2 tablespoons oil

½ teaspoon salt

Chop sweet potato, bell pepper and onion.

In a bowl mix all ingredients together.

Put onto an oven tray and bake at 350°F (180°C) for around 15 minutes or until just getting soft.

Step 2 – Buckwheat

1 cup buckwheat

2 cups boiling water

Add buckwheat and boiling water to a small pot. Bring back to boil, turn down to a simmer and cook for 10 minutes.

Step 3 – Black Beans

12oz (400g) can (2 cups) black beans

1 tablespoon soy sauce or tamari

Put the beans and soy sauce or tamari into a small pot and heat.

Step 4 – Assembly

Honey Ginger Tofu

Mediterranean Vegetables

Toasted Nuts & Seeds

garnish: lime wedges

garnish: cilantro (fresh coriander)

Choose a large serving bowl and create segments of Sweet Potato O'Brien, cooked buckwheat, black beans, Honey Ginger Tofu and Mediterranean Vegetables.

Sprinkle with Toasted Nuts & Seeds and garnish with lime wedges and cilantro.

Honey Ginger Tofu

MAKES 2 X 1 CUP SERVES

20oz (600g) tofu cut into small cubes

1 teaspoon oil

1 tablespoon freshly grated ginger or ginger puree

½ teaspoon turmeric

2 tablespoons liquid honey

¼ teaspoon salt

garnish: sesame seeds

Add diced tofu and oil to a hot medium frying pan.

Grate fresh ginger into the pan. Add turmeric, honey and salt.

Saute for around 15 minutes or until starting to go brown. Stir regularly.

Toasted Nuts & Seeds

MAKES 1 ½ CUPS

½ cup cashew pieces

½ cup pumpkin seeds

½ cup sunflower seeds

¼ cup coconut flakes

Add nuts and seeds to a small hot frying pan and lightly toast for about 7 minutes. Add coconut flakes near the end as they will burn faster than other ingredients.

Tip: You may substitute other nuts and seeds in this recipe. You want 1 ½ cups of nuts and seeds altogether.

Mediterranean Vegetables

MAKES 3 X 1 CUP SERVES

2 cups cherry tomatoes
(mixed colours)

2 cups zucchini (courgette)
(around 2 medium)

1 teaspoon oil

2 cloves garlic crushed

¼ teaspoon salt

garnish: avocado

garnish: cilantro (fresh coriander)

garnish: lime wedges

Cut zucchini in half and slice diagonally into nice big chunks. Put in hot medium frying pan with oil.

Add all remaining ingredients and heat for about 5 minutes or until vegetables are warm and starting to get soft.

To serve, place in a large bowl with a garnish of avocado, cilantro and lime wedges.

Blueberry Power Shake

MAKES 4 X 1 CUP SERVES

1½ cups milk of your choice

2 large bananas

2 cups frozen blueberries

½ avocado

2 tablespoons flax meal (ground linseeds)

2 tablespoons chia seeds

¾ cup cooked quinoa

garnish: blueberries

garnish: chia seeds

Put all ingredients into a blender and blend.

Pour into glasses and let sit to allow the chia seeds to swell slightly.

Add blueberries for garnish.

Tip: If you want a striped look add a couple of tablespoons of milk to the blender at the end and blend for around 1 second. When you pour into a glass you will have streaks of unmixed milk.

Tip: Instead of quinoa you could use brown rice, oats or any other whole grain you have leftover in the fridge.

Three of my
favourite salads
from my cafe
salad bar.

Italian Pumpkin Risotto

Pacifika Coleslaw with Lime Dressing

Beetroot Hummus

Rainbow Bean Salad with Avocado

Strawberry Slushy

Get ready before you start

Jug	Oven	Counter	Ready on stovetop	Plugged in and ready	Preparation required
	Fan bake 350°F (180°C) Oven tray	Chopping board Sharp chefs knife Serving dishes and glasses	Large frying pan	Blender Food processor	3 cups precooked long grain brown rice Precook beetroot if not from packet

Timing

:00	RISOTTO	Prepare and put pumpkin, oil, cashews in oven.
:06	BEANS	Assemble ingredients and make vinaigrette.
:11	HUMMUS	Blend all ingredients and pour into serving dish.
:16	COLESLAW	Assemble ingredients in serving bowl.
:21	RISOTTO	Remove pumpkin from oven and add to other ingredients.
:26	SLUSHY	Blend all ingredients until smooth.
:30	FINISH	Serve and enjoy!

Italian Pumpkin Risotto

MAKES 6 X 1 CUP SERVES

Step 1 – Roast Pumpkin

3 cups pumpkin cubed
½ cup cashew nuts raw
½ teaspoon nutmeg
1 tablespoon oil

Cut pumpkin into 1in (2cm) cubes, put on an oven tray and mix with cashew nuts, nutmeg and oil.

Bake for 20 minutes at 350°F (180°C) or until pumpkin is soft but not mushy.

Step 2 – Cook Rice

3 cups cooked long grain brown rice (or to cook use 1 cup rice and 2 cups hot water)

Cook rice or use pre-cooked from the fridge.

Warm cooked rice in a large frying pan.

Add roasted pumpkin & cashew mixture.

Step 3 – Add Other Ingredients

2 cups frozen green peas
½ red onion diced
½ teaspoon salt
1 tablespoon liquid honey
1 teaspoon mixed herbs

Add peas, red onion, salt, honey, mixed herbs to pan and combine all ingredients together.

Step 4 – Garnish & serve

optional: tahini
optional: pistachio nuts

Drizzle with tahini and top with pistachio nuts to serve.

Pacifika Coleslaw with Lime Dressing

This is a lovely coleslaw bursting with Pacific flavours of lime and coconut.
MAKES 8 X 1 CUP SERVES

3 cups sliced purple cabbage

3 cups grated carrot

2 tablespoons chopped Italian parsley

garnish: 2 tablespoons coconut flakes

LIME DRESSING :

1 tablespoon olive oil

¼ teaspoon salt

4 tablespoons lime juice (around 2 limes)

1 tablespoon liquid honey

Use the slicing attachment of your food processor to slice the cabbage, and your grating attachment to grate the carrot (or use your knife and a handgrater).

Add to serving platter.

Add Italian parsley.

Combine all dressing ingredients in a small bowl and drizzle over the top.

Garnish with coconut flakes.

Beetroot Hummus

Serve with rice crackers or vegetable sticks.
MAKES 2 CUPS

2 tablespoons tahini (sesame seed paste)

3 cloves garlic

12oz (400g) can chickpeas (garbanzo beans) drained

1 teaspoon ground cumin

2 medium beetroot precooked

½ teaspoon salt

2 tablespoons lemon juice (around 1 lemon)

up to ½ cup of water if needed

garnish: Italian parsley

Put all ingredients in food processor and process until smooth. You can also use a stick blender.

Taste and add more water, salt or lemon juice as required.

Garnish with some finely chopped Italian parsley.

Rainbow Bean Salad with Avocado

MAKES 6 X 1 CUP SERVES

12oz (400g) can pinto beans

12oz (400g) can chickpeas (garbanzo beans)

2 cups cherry tomatoes (mixed colours)

1 cup celery roughly chopped

1 cup green bell pepper (capsicum) roughly diced

¼ cup red onion diced small

½ avocado diced

½ cup olives pitted

¼ cup Basic Vinaigrette

garnish: Italian parsely

Add pinto beans, chickpeas, cherry tomatoes, celery, bell pepper and red onion to a large bowl .

Add cubed avocado and olives and mix through with your fingers.

Pour vinaigrette over the salad and garnish with the parsley.

Tip: For this salad you can use any combination of beans and colourful vegetables.

Tip: Green is the one fresh colour that can transform a meal, which is why it is used as a garnish on so many dishes.

Basic Vinaigrette

I prefer using lemon juice instead of vinegar
MAKES ¼ CUP

1 tablespoon olive oil

2 tablespoons lemon juice (around 1 lemon)

1 tablespoon liquid honey

¼ teaspoon salt

¼ cup Italian parsley finely chopped

1 clove garlic crushed

Combine vinaigrette ingredients in a small bowl or cup and stir. When ready to serve, stir and pour the vinaigrette over the salad.

Strawberry Slushy

This combination of strawberries and lemon is very refreshing.
SERVES 4

2 cups frozen strawberries

1 tablespoon lemon juice
(around ½ lemon)

2 tablespoons liquid honey

lemon zest

½ cup water

Add all ingredients to blender and blend until smooth.

If blender is not processing smoothly add more water (up to 1 cup total).

Serve immediately.

Here are
some unique
and different
international
dishes you will
love to try!

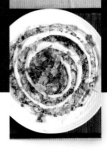

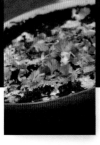

Okonomiyaki (Japanese Pancake)

Hungarian Beetroot & Lentil Borscht

Russian Olivier Salad

Refreshing Citrus Water

Get ready before you start

Jug	Oven	Counter	Ready on stovetop	Plugged in and ready	Preparation required
Boiling with 8 cups of water		Chopping board Sharp chefs knife Serving dishes and glasses	Large pot 1 medium frying pan 1 medium pot	Blender or stick blender Food processor	

Timing

:00	BORSCHT	Saute onion, seeds, garlic, oil.
:03	SALAD	Dice potatoes and put on to boil.
:06	BORSCHT	Grate potatoes, beetroot, carrots and add to onion mix.
:10	PANCAKE	Make batter, chop vegetables, combine and put in hot frying pan.
:14	SALAD	Mix all salad ingredients together.
:18	AIOLI	Blend all ingredients together and pour in serving bowl.
:22	PANCAKE	Flip pancake onto plate and back into pan.
:27	BORSCHT	Add coconut milk.
:28	CITRUS	Assemble all ingredients.
:30	FINISH	Serve and enjoy!

Okonomiyaki (Japanese Pancake)

This is a large savoury pancake usually made with white flour and meat. Try this healthy version!
MAKES 2 LARGE PANCAKES

....

Step 1 – Make Batter

1 cup chickpea (besan) flour
¾ cup water
½ teaspoon salt
½ tablespoon ginger puree

Mix the batter ingredients together in a small bowl.

....

Step 2 – Cut Vegetables

4 cups thinly sliced vegetables:
- cabbage
- red onion
- carrot
- scallions (spring onions)
- mushroom finely diced

Slice the vegetables thinly or use a food processor with a slicer blade.

....

Step 3 – Cook

oil for frying

Heat a non-stick frying pan with a little oil.

In a large bowl, mix ½ cup of the batter with 2 cups of the vegetable mix.

Put the mix in the pan and flatten down. It will need to be flattened a few times as the cabbage reduces in size.

....

Step 4 – Flip then Serve

garnish: sweet chilli sauce
garnish: Cashew & Lemon Aioli
garnish: sesame seeds
garnish: cilantro (fresh coriander)

To flip the pancake put a plate on top, turn upside down and then slide the pancake back into the pan.

Serve with swirls of sauce, aioli, sprinkles of sesame seeds and cilantro.

....

Hungarian Beetroot & Lentil Borscht

A borscht is normally a soup. I love this lentil version of this dish.
MAKES 10 X 1 CUP SERVES

Step 1 – Saute Onions

1½ cups onion finely sliced
(around 1 onion)
3 cloves garlic crushed
2 tablespoons fennel seeds
1 tablespoon oil

In a large pot saute the onion, garlic, fennel seeds and oil for 5 minutes or until the onion is soft.

Step 2 – Grate Vegetables

3 cups grated beetroot
(around 3 beetroot)
3 cups grated potatoes
(around 2 potatoes)
3 cups grated carrot
(around 3 medium carrots)

Using a hand grater or food processor, grate the beetroot, potatoes and carrots.

Add to the onion mix.

Step 3 – Add Lentils

4 cups boiling water
12oz (400g) can brown lentils
1 teaspoon salt
optional: 1 tablespoon crushed chilli paste

Add water, lentils, salt and optional chilli paste and simmer for 20 minutes.

Step 4 – Finish

7oz (200ml) coconut cream
garnish: coconut milk
garnish: cilantro
(fresh coriander) chopped

Using a stick blender blend around one third of the mixture. Alternatively take out ⅓ of the mixture and blend in a blender.

Stir in coconut milk, reserving some for garnish. Garnish with cilantro and coconut milk.

Russian Olivier Salad

A Russian friend introduced me to this salad, explaining that in Russia it is usually eaten at every celebration meal.
MAKES 7 X 1 CUP SERVES

4 cups potatoes diced ½in (1cm) (around 3 potatoes)

1 cup frozen peas

1 cup carrot finely diced

1 cup pickled gherkins finely diced

½ cup capers pickled

½ cup red onion finely diced (around ½ medium onion)

1 cup cucumber finely diced

1 teaspoon salt

½ cup Cashew & Lemon Aioli

1 cup dill or other fresh herbs of your choice, roughly chopped

garnish: fresh dill chopped

garnish: Cashew Lemon Aioli

Place potatoes in a large pot. Cover with boiling water and cook for around 10 minutes or until the potato is just soft.

Drain and cool with cold water.

Combine potato with all remaining ingredients in serving bowl and mix using your hands.

Tip: Try to cut the vegetables approximately the same size.

Tip: If you are not serving straight away, mix everything except the dressing and mix in just before serving

Tip: The frozen peas should not need cooking and will defrost quickly with the warm potato. If you are using cold potato you may need to put the peas in some hot water for a couple of minutes.

Cashew & Lemon Aioli

MAKES 1 CUP

1 ½ cups cashew nuts raw

1 clove garlic

2 teaspoons ground coriander

1 tablespoon seeded mustard

4 tablespoons lemon juice (around 2 lemons)

½ cup water

¼ teaspoon salt

optional: 1 teaspoon sweet chilli sauce (or chopped chilli)

Place all ingredients into blender and blend until smooth and creamy.

If needed, add a little more water to achieve the perfect blending consistency.

Refreshing Citrus Water

MAKES 6 CUPS

3 different types of citrus fruit such as:

- – grapefruit
- – blood orange
- – lemon
- – orange
- – lime

Fill jug about 1/3 full of ice and top up with about 3 cups of water.

Cut 1/3 off each piece of citrus and squeeze the juice into the jug.

Cut approximately 4 slices from each type of citrus and place in jug, ready to serve.

Tip: Use different colours of citrus fruit if available.

Episode
34

My absolute favourite ingredients brought together in one amazing salad.

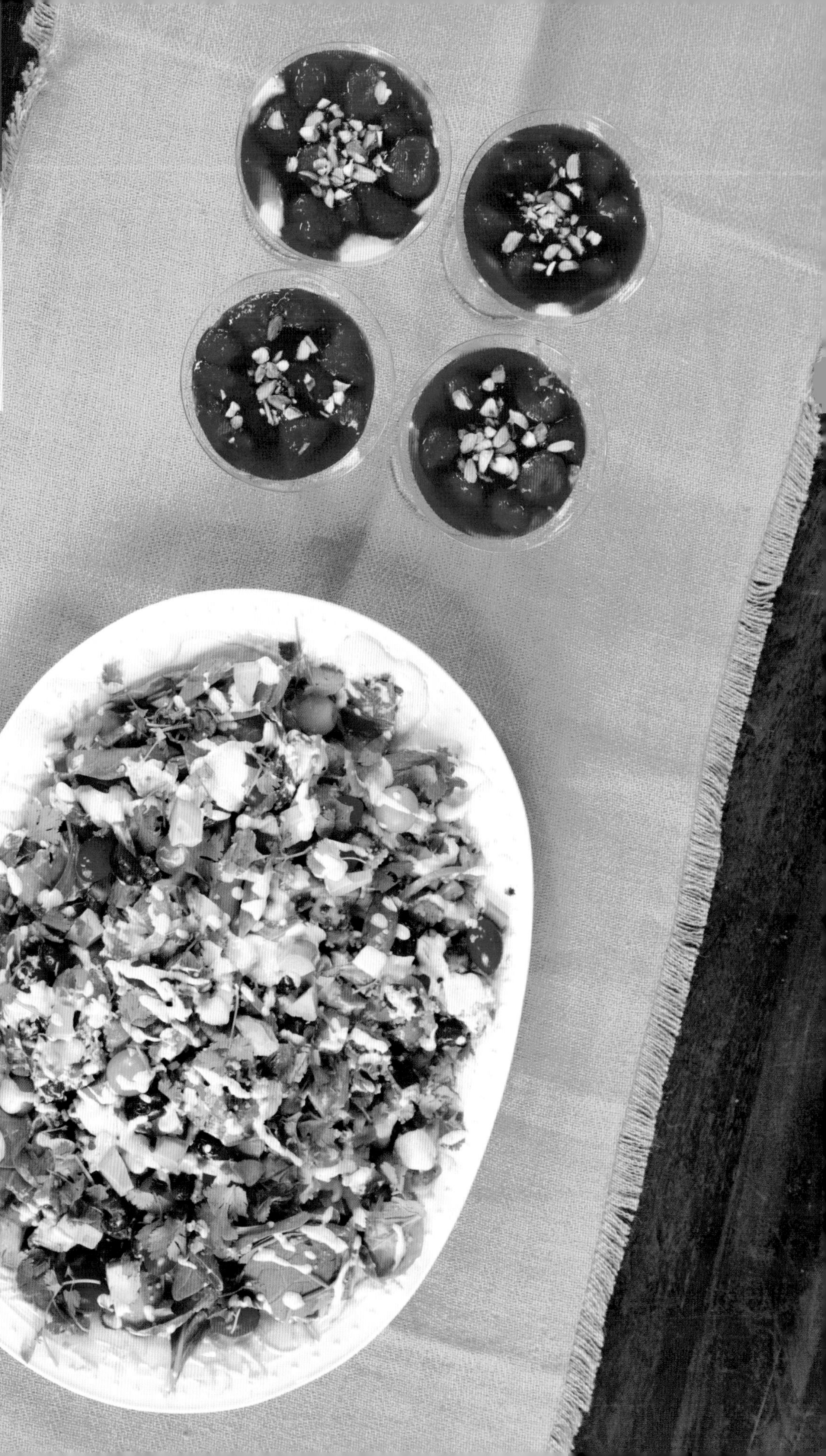

**Revive Super
Salad Mingle**

**Creamy
Strawberry
Parfait**

Get ready before you start

Jug	Oven	Counter	Ready on stovetop	Plugged in and ready	Preparation required
Boiling with 2 cups of water	Fan bake 350°F (180°C)	Chopping board	Small frying pan	Blender or stick blender	
	Oven tray	Sharp chefs knife	Medium frying pan		
		Serving dishes and glasses	Medium pot		

Timing

:00	PARFAIT	Make the base and place in fridge.
:05	BUTTERNUT	Cube butternut, mix with salt, oil, orange juice and place in oven.
:08	VEGES/TOFU	Put quinoa on to boil. Put tofu in hot pan with oil.
:11	SALAD	Chop vegetables and assemble on serving plate.
:14	TOFU	Add honey, ginger and Thai curry paste to hot pan.
:17	PARFAIT	Put fruit into small pan to defrost.
:20	AIOLI	Blend all ingredients in blender.
:23	PARFAIT	Make fruit topping.
:26	SALAD	Assemble all components, including butternut, tofu and quinoa.
:30	FINISH	Serve and enjoy!

Revive Super Salad Mingle

MAKES 10 X 1 CUP SERVES

Step 1 – Roast Butternut

3 cups butternut cubed

1 tablespoon oil

½ teaspoon salt

juice of ½ an orange (around 2 tablespoons)

Cut butternut into ½in (1cm) cubes (do not peel) and mix together in a medium bowl with oil, salt and orange juice.

Place on an oven tray and put in oven at 350°F (180°C) for 20 minutes or until just soft.

Step 2 – Assemble Salad

3 cups baby spinach

2 cups sugar snap peas

2 cups cherry tomatoes

12 asparagus tips raw

1 orange bell pepper (capsicum)

20 kalamata olives pitted

½ avocado cubed

Thai Pan-Fried Tofu

Freshly Cooked Quinoa

Cashew & Lime Aioli

juice of 1 lemon

Put large handful of baby spinach as a base on a serving plate.

Add sugar snap peas, cherry tomatoes and raw asparagus tips.

Add finely sliced bell pepper, olives and avocado.

Top the salad with roasted butternut, Freshly Cooked Quinoa, Thai Pan-Fried Tofu and drizzle with Cashew & Lime Aioli.

Squeeze lemon juice over top.

Cashew & Lime Aioli

MAKES 1 CUP

1½ cups cashew nuts raw

1 clove garlic

2 teaspoons ground coriander

1 tablespoon seeded mustard

4 tablespoons lime juice (around 2 limes)

½ cup water

¼ teaspoon salt

optional: 1 teaspoon sweet chilli sauce or chilli paste

Place all ingredients into blender and blend until smooth and creamy.

Add more water if needed to achieve smooth blending consistency.

Freshly Cooked Quinoa

MAKES 2 X 1 CUP SERVES

1 cup quinoa

2 cups boiling water

In a medium pot add 1 cup quinoa to 2 cups boiling water.

Simmer on low heat for 12–15 minutes with the lid on until water has been absorbed. Do not stir.

Thai Pan-Fried Tofu

MAKES 3 CUPS

10oz (300g) tofu cubed

1 tablespoon oil

1 tablespoon liquid honey

1 tablespoon ginger puree

1 teaspoon Thai curry paste (red or green)

In a hot pan saute the tofu and oil.

Toss or stir every couple of minutes until starting to brown.

In a cup mix honey, ginger and Thai curry paste and stir through the tofu.

Ccook for another minute to allow the tofu to soak up the flavours.

Creamy Strawberry Parfait

A special glass can make this look very decadent.
MAKES 4 X 1 CUP SERVES

. . . .

Step 1 – Make the base

1 tablespoon coconut oil

1 cup cashew nuts raw

1 cup water

1 tablespoon liquid honey

Melt the coconut oil.

Combine all base ingredients into a blender and blend until smooth.

Pour base into parfait glasses and place in fridge.

. . . .

Step 2 – Start the topping

1 cup frozen or fresh strawberries

Heat strawberries in a small pan.

. . . .

Step 3 – Add Thickening Ingredients

1 teaspoon arrowroot (or 2 teaspoons cornstarch/cornflour)

2 tablespoons cold water

2 tablespoons liquid honey

Mix arrowroot, water and honey in a cup and pour over the berries. Keep stirring until you have a nice thick mixture.

. . . .

Step 4 – Finish & garnish

Garnish: pistachio nut pieces

Pour berry mixture over the base ingredients in the glasses. Refrigerate to firm and cool.

Garnish with chopped pistachios.

. . . .

Try these lovely finger food dishes, they are really easy!

Vegetable Sticks with Creamy Basil Hummus

Mini Corn & Cilantro Fritters with Avocado Salsa

Crispy Italian Bruschetta

Energiser Smoothie

Get ready before you start

Jug	Oven	Counter	Ready on stovetop	Plugged in and ready	Preparation required
Boiling with 1 cup of water	Fan bake 350°F (180°C) Oven tray	Chopping board Sharp chefs knife Serving dishes and glasses	Medium frying pan	Blender or stick blender	

Timing

:00	FRITTERS	Saute onion and make batter. Start to fry.
:08	SALSA	Combine all ingredients together.
:12	FRITTERS	Flip fritters.
:14	BRUSCHETTA	Prepare bread and put in oven. Make tomato/olive mix.
:17	VEGE STICKS	Blend all hummus ingredients until smooth.
:21	FRITTERS	Flip fritters and start another batch.
:23	VEGE STICKS	Cut vege sticks and arrange in serving glasses.
:25	FRITTERS	Flip fritters.
:27	SMOOTHIE	Blend all ingredients and pour into glasses.
:30	FINISH	Serve and enjoy!

Vegetable Sticks

SERVES 4

10 stalks asparagus

1/3 red bell pepper (capsicum)

1 carrot peeled

2 stalks celery

2 cups Basil Hummus

Break the woody ends off the asparagus stalks.

Slice bell pepper, carrot and celery into good-sized dipping sticks.

Pour Basil Hummus into serving glasses and arrange 2-3 sticks of each vegetable in each glass.

Creamy Basil Hummus

MAKES 4 X ½ CUP SERVES

1 can chickpeas (garbanzo beans) drained

1 cup basil leaves

½ teaspoon salt

2 tablespoons lemon juice (around 1 lemon)

2 tablespoons tahini

1 clove garlic

up to ½ cup water

Blend all ingredients together until smooth and creamy.

Add water as needed to make a thick paste but thin enough that the blender still turns around.

Mini Corn & Cilantro Fritters

MAKES 10 LARGE FRITTERS

1 medium onion finely diced

1 tablespoon oil

1 cup chickpea (besan) flour

up to ½ cup water

2 cups frozen or canned whole kernel corn (no need to defrost if frozen)

½ teaspoon salt

1 tablespoon sweet chilli sauce or fresh chopped chilli

½–1 cup cilantro (fresh coriander)

oil (for frying)

Saute onion in oil until soft.

Add chickpea flour to large mixing bowl and stir in water.

Add corn and more water, if needed, to create a pourable but thick batter.

Add salt, sweet chilli sauce, cilantro and sauted onions.

To make mini fritters drop about 1 tablespoon of batter into pan. Cook about 2-3 minutes each side. Serve with small blobs of avocado salsa on top.

Avocado Salsa

MAKES 1½ CUPS

1 avocado

¼ red onion

1 red tomato

1 teaspoon salt

1 clove garlic crushed

2 tablespoons lemon juice (around 1 lemon)

½–1 cup cilantro (fresh coriander)

½ tablespoon olive oil

Chop avocado finely into small cubes.

Finely chop red onion and tomato and add to bowl.

Add remaining ingredients together.

Crispy Italian Bruschetta

SERVES 8

1 wholegrain breadstick

1 tablespoon olive oil

2 cloves garlic crushed

4 tomatoes (mixed colours)

1 handful fresh basil leaves

10 kalamata olives pitted

1 clove garlic crushed

½ teaspoon salt

garnish: Italian parsley

Cut bread into ½in (1cm) thick slices and lay out on a baking sheet.

Put olive oil in a small bowl, add garlic and stir.

Brush oil mixture onto bread slices.

Grill (broil) in the top of the oven for 5 minutes or until slightly brown. Don't let the garlic burn

Cut the tomatoes, basil leaves and olives as small as you can and put in a bowl. Add garlic and salt.

Place the crispy bread on a serving dish.

Put the tomato mixture on top of the hot bread pieces and serve immediately. Garnish with Italian parsley.

Energiser Smoothie

This smoothie is very refreshing and a great cafe favourite!
MAKES 4 SERVES

2 oranges

1 large banana

2 cups frozen strawberries

Peel the skin off the oranges with a knife and remove seeds.

Put oranges and banana in the bottom of a blender, followed by the strawberries on top.

Blend until smooth.

Try these zoodles for a delicious raw noodle!

Alfredo Sauce

Zoodles

Carrot & Parsnip Smash

Parmeshew Cheese

Kiwi, Banana & Ginger Smoothie

Get ready before you start

Jug	Oven	Counter	Ready on stovetop	Plugged in and ready	Preparation required
Boiling with 6 cups of water		Chopping board	1 large frying pan	Blender or stick blender	
		Sharp chefs knife	1 large pot		
		Spiraliser			
		Serving dishes			

Timing

:00	SMASH	Chop carrot and parsnip and start to cook.
:04	ALFREDO	Saute, oil, onion, garlic, bell peppers, mushrooms, asparagus.
:09	ALFREDO	Make sauce and add to pan.
:14	ZOODLES	Put zucchini through the spiraliser. Add dressing and garnish.
:19	CHEESE	Blend all ingredients and put in small serving bowl.
:24	SMASH	Add milk, nutmeg, salt, parsley and mash roughly.
:27	SMOOTHIE	Blend all ingredients together.
:30	FINISH	Serve and enjoy!

Alfredo Sauce

MAKES 6 X 1 CUP SERVES

Step 1 – Cut Vegetables

1 cup red onion diced
1 red bell pepper (capsicum)
1 yellow bell pepper (capsicum)
1 orange bell pepper (capsicum)

Cut onion and bell peppers into ½in (1cm) chunks.

Step 2 – Saute Vegetables

10 mushrooms (6oz /200g)
1 tablespoon oil
2 cloves garlic crushed
8 asparagus stalks

Slice the mushrooms thickly.

Add oil, garlic, onion, bell peppers and mushrooms to a hot pan.

Break asparagus stalks in half and add the tips to the pan.

Saute until vegetables are just soft.

Step 3 – Make Sauce

1 ½ cups (7oz/200g) tofu
1 cup rice, soy or almond milk
½ teaspoon ginger puree
2 tablespoons nutritional yeast flakes
1 teaspoon salt
1 tablespoon liquid honey
1 clove garlic

Add all sauce ingredients to a blender and blend until smooth.

Step 4 – Garnish

garnish: chives chopped

Pour sauce into the frying pan and cook gently until heated through.

Zoodles

An inexpensive spiraliser is all you need to create this healthy take on noodles!
MAKES 4 X 1 CUP SERVES

3 zucchini (courgettes)

¼ teaspoon chilli paste

1 teaspoon liquid honey

1 tablespoon olive oil

¼ teaspoon salt

juice of 1 lemon

garnish: cherry tomatoes (mixed colours) cut into quarters

Cut the ends off the zucchini and make noodles by putting through a spiraliser machine going directly into the serving dish.

To make the dressing, add remaining ingredients to a small bowl and stir to combine.

Pour dressing over zoodles and add quartered cherry tomatoes to garnish.

Carrot & Parsnip Smash

MAKES 4 X 1 CUP SERVES

4 carrots sliced

3 large parsnips diced into large chunks

½ cup soy milk

½ teaspoon salt

¼ cup Italian parsley chopped

1 teaspoon nutmeg

garnish: Italian parsley

Put carrots and parsnip into pot. Cover with boiling water and cook for about 10 minutes or until just soft.

Drain.

Roughly mash all ingredients together, leaving some chunky bits.

Parmeshew Cheese

A quick flavour booster and a healthful alternative to Parmesan cheese.
MAKES 1 CUP

1 cup cashew nuts raw

2 tablespoons nutritional yeast flakes

Put ingredients into a blender and blend for 30 seconds or until you get a bread crumb texture. The time will depend on your blender.

You may have to use a spoon to take the mixture off the sides of the blender and re-blend to get it consistent.

Tip: This will store in your fridge for weeks. Keep some on hand to spice up your food!

Kiwi, Banana & Ginger Smoothie

SERVES 4

MILK:

¼ cup almonds

1 ¼ cups water

SMOOTHIE:

4 kiwifruit peeled

2 frozen bananas

1 tablespoon fresh ginger, peeled and finely chopped

garnish: slices of kiwifruit

Make almond milk by blending water and almonds together. (Alternatively use store-bought almond, rice or soy milk).

Put kiwifruit, banana and ginger into the blender with the milk and blend until smooth.

Tip: When making smoothies you want one of the fruit ingredients frozen and the other not. When using frozen berries use fresh banana. When using soft fruit such as kiwi in this recipe, use frozen banana.

This soup, salad and smoothie makes for a delicious and colourful combination.

Honey Mustard Potato Salad

Minty Pea Soup with Wholemeal Croutons

Seedy Crackers

Black Cherry Smoothie

Get ready before you start

Jug	Oven	Counter	Ready on stovetop	Plugged in and ready	Preparation required
Boiling with 5 cups of water	Fan bake 350°F (180°C)	Chopping board	Medium pot with high sides	Blender or stick blender	
	3 oven trays	Sharp chefs knife			
		Serving dishes and glasses			

Timing

:00	SALAD	Put potatoes on to roast.
:04	CRACKERS	Blend seeds, mix with water and put into oven.
:08	SOUP	Saute onion, oil, garlic.
:12	SOUP	Make croutons and put in oven. Add peas and boiling water to pot.
:16	SALAD	Make dressing. Assemble salad ingredients and add.
:20	CRACKERS	Remove crackers and croutons from oven.
:22	SOUP	Half blend the soup and add cashew cream, salt and mint.
:27	SMOOTHIE	Add all ingredients to blender and blend.
:30	FINISH	Serve and enjoy!

Honey Mustard Potato Salad

A cafe favourite!
MAKES 8 X 1 CUP SERVES

Step 1 – Prepare Potatoes

4 cups small potatoes halved or
regular potatoes
2 teaspoons oil

On a baking tray mix potatoes and oil together.

Place in oven and bake at 350°F (180°C) for 20 minutes or until
almost soft.

Step 2 – Make the Dressing

3 tablespoons tahini
1 tablespoon liquid honey
2 tablespoons seeded mustard
3 tablespoons lemon juice
½ teaspoon salt

Mix all dressing ingredients in a cup.

Step 3 – Prepare Vegetables

4 cups baby spinach
¼ cup chopped mint
1 red bell pepper (capsicum)
thinly sliced

Lay the spinach and mint on your serving dish. Mix the roasted potatoes
with ½ cup dressing, reserving some for garnish. Add potato mix and
sliced bell pepper on top of the bed of spinach and mint.

Step 4 – Garnish

½ cup pecans
garnish: mint
garnish: dressing

Garnish with pecans and extra mint. Drizzle remaining dressing over top
to serve.

Minty Pea Soup

This is my favourite soup of all time. Well, until the next one comes along...
MAKES 6 X 1 CUP SERVES

1 cup onion roughly chopped (around 1 onion)

3 cloves garlic crushed

2 teaspoons oil

¾ cup cashew nuts raw

1 cup hot water

3 cups frozen peas

4 cups boiling water

1 teaspoon salt

¼ cup fresh mint

garnish: mint

Saute onion, garlic, oil in a medium pot. I recommend you use a pot with high sides so the stick blender can blend without mess.

In a blender, blend cashew nuts and hot water until smooth and creamy.

Add frozen peas to pot. Add boiling water and cook for 5 minutes. Don't overcook or peas will go brown.

Add cashew cream to the soup and reserve a little for garnish.

Add salt and mint and blend the soup with a stick blender until smooth.

Transfer to a serving dish and serve with a garnish of mint, cashew cream and warm croutons on top.

Tip: When purchasing peas, be aware that most "minted peas" only contain mint flavouring, not actual mint.

Wholemeal Croutons

MAKES 4 X 1 CUP SERVES

2 wholemeal buns or 4 slices toast slice wholemeal bread

1 teaspoon oil

¼ teaspoon salt

Cut bread into ½ in(1cm) cubes and place on baking tray. Sprinkle salt over top and spray lightly with oil.

Bake at 350°F (180°C) for 5 minutes or until crispy on the outside (but not hard all the way through).

Seedy Crackers

SERVES 4

½ cup pumpkin seeds
½ cup chia seeds
½ cup sesame seeds
½ cup sunflower seeds
1 teaspoon ground cumin
1 teaspoon mixed herbs
½ teaspoon salt
½ teaspoon chilli paste or sweet chilli sauce
5 tablespoons water

Preheat oven to 350°F (180°C). Place all seeds in the food processor and pulse to a flour consistency.

Mix together with all remaining ingredients and spoon onto a baking tray lined with parchment (baking) paper.

Place sheet of parchment paper on top and flatten mixture out to approximately 4mm thick. Peel paper off.

Lightly spray oil on top to prevent burning and bake in oven for 15 minutes or until golden.

Store in an airtight container.

Tip: You can add any flavour you like to this. I have also made one at cooking demonstrations where the seeds aren't blended, but it needs to sit for about 30 minutes before rolling out so that it holds together.

Black Cherry Smoothie

This amazing smoothie is made with my favourite frozen fruit!
SERVES 4

2 cups frozen black cherries
2 large ripe bananas
2 cups soy or rice milk unsweetened
3 tablespoons liquid honey
optional: 1 cup ice

Put all ingredients into a blender and blend.

Garnish with extra cherries and serve immediately.

This Indian Curry Feast will surprise you with how good healthy food can taste!

Tofu Tikka Masala

Fruity Rice Pilaf

Refreshing Cucumber & Zucchini Salad

Chana Saag

Raspberry Lassi

Get ready before you start

Jug	Oven	Counter	Ready on stovetop	Plugged in and ready	Preparation required
Boiling with 6 cups of water		Chopping board Sharp chefs knife Serving dishes and glasses	Small frying pan Large pan Large pot	Blender or stick blender	4 cups precooked brown rice

Timing

:00	PILAF	Add boiling water to dried fruit and soak.
:02	MASAL/SAAG	Start 2 pans sauteing with onion, garlic, oil, ginger.
:07	MASALA	Add cumin, paprika, chilli powder, turmeric, clove powder.
:10	SAAG	Add fennel seeds, coriander to pan. Pour boiling water on spinach.
:12	MASALA	Add tomatoes and tomato paste.
:15	PILAF	Saute onion, oil, celery. Add spices, rice, peas and drained fruit.
:19	SALAD	Assemble salad.
:23	MASALA	Add tofu and coconut milk, honey and salt.
:26	SAAG	Add spinach, coconut milk. Blend smooth. Add chickpeas and heat.
:30	FINISH	Serve and enjoy!

Tofu Tikka Masala

MAKES 8 X 1 CUP SERVES

....

Step 1 – Onion Mix

2 teaspoons oil

1½ cups onion finely diced (around 1 large onion)

2 cloves garlic crushed

1 tablespoon ginger puree

In a pot or pan saute the oil, onion, garlic and ginger for 5 minutes or until the onion is soft.

....

Step 2 – Add Spices

1 teaspoon cumin

1 teaspoon smoked paprika

1 teaspoon clove powder

1 teaspoon turmeric

$^{1}/_{8}$ teaspoon chilli powder

Add the spices and stir around for 30 seconds to activate the flavours.

....

Step 3 – Add Tomatoes

2 x 12oz (400g) cans tomatoes crushed

6 tablespoons tomato paste

Add the tomatoes and tomato paste and heat until just bubbling.

....

Step 4 – Finish & Garnish

7oz (200g) tofu diced

2 tablespoons liquid honey

½ teaspoon salt

7oz (200ml) coconut cream

garnish: cilantro (fresh coriander)

garnish: coconut cream

Add the tofu, honey, salt and coconut cream and heat gently.

Garnish with cilantro and a drizzle of coconut cream.

....

Fruity Rice Pilaf

MAKES 5 X 1 CUP SERVES

3 cups boiling water

1½ cups mixed dried fruit: cranberries, raisins, golden raisins, figs diced, apricots diced

½ red onion finely diced

1 stalk celery finely diced

1 teaspoon oil

¼ teaspoon cardamom powder

1 teaspoon cumin seeds

¼ teaspoon cinnamon

4 cups cooked brown rice

1 cup frozen peas

½ teaspoon turmeric

½ teaspoon salt

garnish: mint

Put dried fruit into a bowl and cover with boiling water.

Leave to soak for 10 minutes to allow fruit to become plump and juicy.

Saute onion, celery and oil.

Add cardamom, cumin seeds and cinnamon and stir for about 30 seconds.

Add rice and frozen peas.

Drain fruit and add to pan.

Add turmeric and salt and warm dish through.

Garnish with chopped mint.

Refreshing Cucumber & Zucchini Salad

MAKES 3 X 1 CUP SERVES

1 cucumber

1 zucchini (courgette)

1 cup dill chopped

2 tablespoons lemon juice (around 1 lemon)

½ teaspoon salt

dash of olive oil

3 red cherry tomatoes halved

3 yellow cherry tomatoes halved

Use a potato peeler to make ribbons of cucumber and zucchini.

When you get to the seeds in the middle turn over and peel the other side.

Add chopped dill, lemon juice, salt and olive oil and mix all together. Add cherry tomatoes on top.

 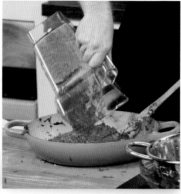 

Chana Saag

Blend all these tasty ingredients together and you know it will taste good!
MAKES 6 X 1 CUP SERVES

1½ cups onion sliced thinly (around 1 onion)

3 cloves garlic crushed

1 tablespoon ginger puree

1 tablespoon oil

1 teaspoon fennel seeds

1 tablespoon cumin

3 cups frozen spinach (around 20oz/600g)

1 tablespoon liquid honey

½ teaspoon salt

7oz (200g) coconut cream

12oz (400g) can chickpeas (garbanzo beans)

garnish: red bell pepper (capsicum) finely chopped

In a pot or pan saute the onion, garlic, ginger and oil for 5 minutes or until the onion is soft.

Add fennel seeds and cumin and stir for 30 seconds to activate the flavours.

Put frozen spinach in a bowl and pour boiling water over to thaw.

Add the honey, salt and coconut cream.

Blend the mixture using a stick blender, or by putting it all into a blender. Make sure you blend it well, you do not want any stringy bits.

Put back in the pan or pot, add the chickpeas and heat until just bubbling.

Serve with a garnish of some finely chopped red capsicum.

Tip: Spinach can turn a black colour when overcooked. Make sure you add spinach near the end and serve soon after cooking.

Raspberry Lassi

SERVES 4

2 cups frozen raspberries

1 cup or 6oz (170g) coconut yoghurt (optional)

1 cup almond, rice or soy milk

1½ tablespoons liquid honey

garnish: fresh raspberries

garnish: mint leaves

Blend all ingredients in a blender.

Add a little more milk if needed to achieve smooth blending.

Pour into nice serving glasses and garnish with fresh raspberries and mint.

A tasty frittata without eggs, plus two great accompaniments!

Mini Butternut Frittatas

Sweet Potato Hash

Panzanella

Cranberry Bliss Balls

Wild Berry Iced Water

Get ready before you start

Jug	Oven	Counter	Ready on stovetop	Plugged in and ready	Preparation required
Boiling with 7 cups of water	Fan bake 350°F (180°C) Oven tray Muffin tray	Chopping board Sharp chefs knife Serving dishes	Medium frying pan Large pot	Blender Food processor	

Timing

:00	FRITTATA	Prepare butternut and put in oven.
:04	HASH	Prepare potatoes and sweet potatoes and put on to boil.
:09	PANZANELLA	Prepare bread and put in oven.
:12	FRITTATA	Saute onion, bell pepper, oil. Blend all other ingredients.
:14	PANZANELLA	Take butternut and bread out of oven.
:15	FRITTATA	Combine ingredients, add to prepared muffin tin and place in oven.
:19	PANZANELLA	Put green beans in potato pot of boiling water.
:20	BLISS BALLS	Whizz all ingredients in the food processor and roll the balls.
:27	HASH/SALAD	Drain potatoes and mash roughly – add salt. Assemble salad.
:30	FINISH	Add all Berry Iced Water ingredients to jug. Serve and enjoy!

Mini Butternut Frittatas

MAKES 6 FRITTATAS

....

Step 1 – Roast Pumpkin

2–3 cups pumpkin or butternut squash diced into small ½in (1cm) cubes

oil spray or 1 tablespoon oil

Line a baking tray with parchment (baking) paper. Add diced pumpkin and spray lightly with oil.

Bake at 350°F (180°C) for around 15 minutes or until just getting soft.

....

Step 2 – Saute Vegetables

2 teaspoons oil

1 cup red onion sliced (around 1 small onion)

1 cup red bell pepper (capsicum) roughly diced

In a pot or pan saute the oil, onion and bell pepper for 5 minutes or until the onion is soft.

....

Step 3 – Make "Egg" Mix

¼ cup chickpea (besan) flour

12oz (350g) firm tofu

1 teaspoon salt

½ teaspoon turmeric

1 tablespoon arrowroot

2 cloves garlic

up to ¼ cup water

Put the chickpea flour, tofu, salt, turmeric, arrowroot and garlic into a blender and blend until you have a smooth batter that is pourable. You may have to add extra water and continue to blend.

....

Step 4 – Finish & Garnish

garnish: thyme

Line each hole in a large muffin tin with parchment paper.

Put the pumpkin and onion mixture in the trays. You want this to almost fill the trays.

Pour the batter mixture over the vegetables.

Tap the tray on your counter to make sure it fills in all the spaces.

You may need to use a knife to gently stir the contents to ensure there are no air gaps.

Put in the oven and bake at 350°F (180°C) for 15-20 minutes or until the frittatas are set but still soft.

Garnish with thyme or other fresh herbs.

....

Sweet Potato Hash

MAKES 5 X 1 CUP SERVES

2 cups potato diced ½in (1cm) (around 1 large potato)

4 cups orange sweet potato (kumara) sliced

7 cups boiling water

1 tablespoon oil

¾ teaspoon salt

garnish: Italian parsley

Chop the potatoes and sweet potato. Make sure you cut the potatoes finely as they will take longer to cook than the sweet potato.

Put the chopped potato, sweet potato and boiling water in a pot, bring back to the boil and simmer for 15 minutes or until soft. Drain.

When cooked mash roughly and stir in the salt.

Garnish with finely chopped parsley.

Panzanella

MAKES 7 X 1 CUP SERVES

5 slices wholegrain bread

spray oil (for baking)

¼ teaspoon salt

1 cup yellow cherry tomatoes smashed

1 cup red cherry tomatoes smashed

10 long green beans cut diagonally

¼ cup Italian parsley

drizzle of olive oil (for dressing)

1 tablespoon lemon juice (around ½ a lemon)

2 cloves garlic crushed

Roughly tear bread into approximately 1in (2cm) pieces onto a baking tray lined with parchment (baking) paper.

Lightly spray with oil and add a sprinkle of salt. Place in oven at 350°F (180°C) for 5 minutes or until just crispy.

Chop the ends off the green beans and cut diagonally into bite-sized pieces. Cook green beans in boiling water for around 3 minutes.

Using your hands and a chopping board squash the cherry tomatoes flat.

Place baked bread, green beans and squashed cherry tomatoes, including the juices, into a serving bowl. Drizzle with olive oil, lemon juice and garlic.

Mix everything together with your hands.

Cranberry Bliss Balls

MAKES 12 BALLS

½ cup dried dates
½ cup dried cranberries
½ cup cashew nuts
½ cup almonds
2 tablespoons carob powder
up to ½ cup water
½ cup shredded coconut

Soak fruit in boiling water for around 5 minutes. This is not essential but will soften the fruit and help your food processor last longer.

Put fruit, nuts, carob and half the water into a food processor and blend until you have a consistent paste.

Add water as needed so you get the balance between a mix that will blend and one that is not too soft.

Pour coconut on a plate.

Spoon out ¼ cup and divide into two so you have ⅛ cup size balls. Roll each into circular balls in your hands and put in the coconut. It is best to do all the rolling together while your hands are sticky.

They will firm up a little when you refrigerate them.

Wild Berry Iced Water

MAKES 6 X 1 CUP SERVES

8 ice cubes

5 cups filtered water

handful frozen blueberries

handful frozen raspberries

3 large strawberries roughly diced

2 sprigs mint

Add ice cubes to serving jug.

Add filtered water, blueberries, raspberries, strawberries and mint and stir lightly.

This is a great pasta and salad combo, with a delicious healthy dessert to top it off!

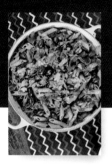

Arrabiata Penne Pasta

Moroccan Carrot Salad

Rocket & Cranberry Salad

Baked Fruity Apples with Cashew Cream

Get ready before you start

Jug	Oven	Counter	Ready on stovetop	Plugged in and ready	Preparation required
Boiling with 3 cups of water	Fan bake 400°F (200°C) Oven tray	Chopping board Sharp chefs knife Serving dishes and glasses	Large frying pan Medium pot	Blender or stick blender Food processor	

Timing

:00	APPLES	Core apples, stuff with fruity spice mix and place in oven.
:06	PASTA	Put pasta on to boil. Saute vegetables.
:13	ROCKET	Assemble salad ingredients. Pour over dressing and garnish.
:17	MOROCCAN	Grate carrots, chop cilantro, make dressing and combine.
:22	PASTA	Add salt, tomatoes, tomato paste, chilli paste and simmer.
:24	APPLES	Blend cashews and water to make cream.
:27	PASTA	Drain pasta and add to pot with spinach and parsley and heat.
:30	FINISH	Serve and enjoy!

Arrabiata Penne Pasta

MAKES 6 X 1 CUP SERVES

Step 1 – Start Pasta

2 ½ cups boiling water
9oz (250g) wholemeal
penne pasta
¹/₈ teaspoon salt

Place penne, water and salt in a medium pot and bring to boil for 8 minutes or cook as per packet instructions.

Step 2 – Start Veges

1 tablespoon olive oil
1 onion chopped finely
4 cloves garlic crushed
1 red bell pepper (capsicum)
2 zucchini (courgettes) diced
1 aubergine (eggplant) finely diced

Saute oil, onion and garlic in a large pan until onion is clear.

Add diced bell pepper, zucchini and aubergine to pan and cook until soft.

Step 3 – Add Flavourings

1 teaspoon salt
12oz (400g) can
tomatoes crushed
1 tablespoon tomato paste
½ teaspoon chilli paste
1 teaspoon liquid honey

Add salt, tomatoes, tomato paste, chilli paste, honey and simmer on high for 5 minutes.

Step 4 – Finish

9oz (250g) baby spinach
½ cup Italian parsley chopped
garnish: Italian parsley
garnish: 20 kalamata olives (pitted)

Drain pasta and add together with baby spinach, parsley and cook gently for a further 2 minutes.

Serve with Italian parsley and olives sprinkled on top.

Moroccan Carrot Salad

MAKES 3 X 1 CUP SERVES

2 large carrots, julienned or
coarsely grated

1 cup chopped cilantro
(fresh coriander)

1 cup Yoghurt Lemon Dressing

Use your food processor to coarsely grate carrots and add to serving dish
with chopped cilantro.

Pour ¾ of the dressing onto the salad and mix together gently with
your hands.

Pour the remaining dressing over top as a garnish.

Yoghurt Lemon Dressing

MAKES 1 CUP

1 cup coconut or soy yoghurt

¼ teaspoon salt

2 teaspoons liquid honey

1 teaspoon cumin

¼ teaspoon turmeric

2 tablespoons lemon juice (around 1 lemon)

Add all dressing ingredients to a small bowl and stir
until well combined.

Rocket & Cranberry Salad

MAKES 3 X 1 CUP SERVES

3 cups baby arugula (rocket)
¼ cup cranberries
¼ cup walnuts
¼ cup toasted sesame seeds
¼ cup Lemon & Honey Dressing

Add arugula to serving dish and top with cranberries and walnuts.

Drizzle Lemon & Honey Dressing over top and sprinkle with toasted sesame seeds.

Lemon & Honey Dressing

MAKES ¼ CUP

1 tablespoon olive oil
1 tablespoon lemon juice (around ½ lemon)
1 tablespoon liquid honey

In a small cup add dressing ingredients and mix until well combined.

Baked Fruity Apples

SERVES 4

4 apples cored

1 cup dried fruit:

½ cup chopped dates

½ cup raisins, apricots or cranberries

2 teaspoons cinnamon

1 teaspoon ginger

½ cup chopped almonds or nut of choice

½ cup boiling water

Heat oven to 400°F (200°C).

In a small bowl mix dried fruit, nuts and spices and a little water.

Core apples and place in a baking dish. Press fruity mix firmly into apples.

Pour hot water onto base of dish and place in oven for 20-30 minutes, until apple is soft, but not mushy.

Serve with cashew cream.

Cashew Cream

MAKES 1 CUP

1 cup cashew nuts raw

1 cup water

Add water and cashews to blender and blend until smooth and creamy.

Here are some of
my favourite
Thai dishes.

Thai Green Curry Chickpeas

Thai Tofu Kebabs

Peanut Satay Sauce

Grilled Fruit

Apple & Cinnamon Cashew Cream

Get ready before you start

Jug	Oven	Counter	Ready on stovetop	Plugged in and ready	Preparation required
Boiling with 5 cups of water	Oven on broil (grill) 475°F (250°C) Oven tray	Chopping board Sharp chefs knife Serving dishes and glasses	Large frying pan Small pot Medium pot Large pan	Blender or stick blender	Chickpeas (garbanzos) precooked and in freezer or use 12oz (400g) can chickpeas

Timing

:00	CURRY	Put rice on to cook. Saute onion and vegetable mix.
:05	KEBABS	Put tofu on skewers in pan.
:08	SATAY	Saute onions, ginger, garlic.
:11	CURRY	Add zucchini and broccoli.
:14	KEBAB	Turn skewers over.
:15	CURRY	Add flavours.
:16	FRUIT	Prepare fruit and place in oven.
:22	SATAY	Add remaining ingredients and stir through.
:25	CURRY	Add coconut cream and chickpeas.
:26	FRUIT	Make cream.
:30	FINISH	Plate up dishes. Spoon satay sauce over kebabs.

Thai Green Curry Chickpeas

MAKES 6 X 1 CUP SERVES

Step 1 – Rice

1 cup long grain brown rice

2 cups boiling water

Put rice and boiling water in pot with the lid on and boil for 20 minutes. Do not stir. If using jasmine brown rice it will take an extra 10 minutes to cook.

Step 2 – Saute Vegetables

1 tablespoon oil

1½ cups onion diced

2 cloves garlic crushed

1 tablespoon ginger puree

1 cup red onion diced

½ red bell pepper (capsicum) diced

2 cups button mushrooms cut in half (around 5oz /150g)

10 long green beans

1 zucchini (courgette) diced

2 cups broccoli florets

Saute oil, onion, garlic, ginger, red onion, bell pepper and mushrooms for 5 minutes or until onion is soft.

Chop ends off beans, cut into bite-sized pieces and add to curry.

Add zucchini and broccoli and saute for a further 5 minutes.

Step 3 – Finish Curry

1 teaspoon turmeric powder

1 tablespoon Thai green curry paste

1½ cups hot water

2 tablespoons liquid honey

1 cup cooked chickpeas (garbanzo beans)

7oz (200ml) coconut cream

1 teaspoon salt

Add the turmeric and stir briefly.

Mix the curry paste with the water in a large cup and pour in.

Heat until it is bubbling.

Add remaining ingredients and heat through.

Serve with the cooked brown rice.

Thai Tofu Kebabs

MAKES 8 KEBABS

18oz (600g) firm tofu cubed
1 tablespoon oil
1 teaspoon salt
8 bamboo skewers
garnish: cilantro (coriander)

Cut tofu into large 1in (2cm) cubes.

Push the skewers through the tofu cubes.

In a non-stick pan saute the tofu and oil for around 10 minutes until golden brown.

Sprinkle with salt.

Drizzle over satay sauce and garnish with cilantro.

Peanut Satay Sauce

MAKES ½ CUP

1 cup onion diced (around 1 medium onion)
4 tablespoons ginger puree
4 cloves garlic crushed
1 tablespoon oil
optional: 1 chilli de-seeded and finely diced
1 teaspoon cumin
1 teaspoon ground coriander
6 tablespoons peanut butter
½ cup hot water
1 tablespoon liquid honey

In a pot or pan saute the onions, ginger, garlic and oil until the onions are clear.

Stir in the optional chilli, cumin and coriander.

In a cup mix the peanut butter with the water so it is a runny paste.

Add the peanut paste and honey to the onion mix. Bring back to the heat while stirring.

You may need to add a little more water to adjust the consistency. However only add small amounts as it does not take much to turn it from a nice thick satay into a runny one.

Grilled Fruit

SERVES 4

1 pineapple sliced, peeled and cored

2 bananas

1 orange sliced with skin on strawberries

blueberries whole

blackberries whole

Place fruit in a baking dish, drizzle with honey and grill for 5 or so minutes, checking regularly.

Serve with Apple & Cinnamon Cashew Cream.

Tip: You can use many different types of fresh fruit for this.

Apple & Cinnamon Cashew Cream

MAKES 1 CUP

1 cup cashew nuts raw

1 cup apple juice

½ teaspoon cinnamon

Put all ingredients into blender and blend until smooth and creamy.

You will love this flavoursome Mexican combination.

Vegetable Nacho Beans

Mexican Guacamole Salad

Soft Corn Tortilla Wedges

Zingy Tomato Salsa

Mango & Raspberry Coconut Ice

Get ready before you start

Jug	Oven	Counter	Ready on stovetop	Plugged in and ready	Preparation required
	Fan bake 350°F (180°C)	Chopping board	Large pan	Blender or stick blender	
	Oven tray	Sharp chefs knife			
		Serving dishes and glasses			

Timing

:00	DESSERT	Take mango and raspberries out of freezer.
:01	NACHOS	Saute onion, oil, garlic, celery, bell pepper, chilli.
:05	SALAD	Combine all ingredients in serving bowl.
:09	GUACAMOLE	Mash avocado, add cilantro, honey, salt, lime, lemon, red onion.
:13	NACHOS	Add kidney beans, butter beans, corn kernels, tomatoes.
:17	TORTILLA	Cut pita into wedges, spray with oil and put in oven.
:20	SALSA	Combine chopped tomatoes, red onion, lime juice, salt, cilantro.
:23	NACHOS	Add crushed tomatoes, grated zucchini and lime juice.
:26	DESSERT	Blend mango, raspberries, lemon, honey, coconut milk.
:30	FINISH	Serve and enjoy!

Vegetable Nacho Beans

MAKES 8 X 1 CUP SERVES

Step 1 – Onion Mix

1 tablespoon oil

1 onion chopped

3 cloves garlic crushed

2 stalks celery sliced

1 orange bell pepper
(capsicum) diced

½ cup cilantro (fresh
coriander) stalks

½ red chilli chopped finely or
1 tablespoon chilli paste

Add oil to saucepan and saute oil, onion, garlic, celery, bell pepper, cilantro stalks and chilli for 5 minutes or until soft.

Step 2 – Beans

12oz (400g) can
tomatoes chopped

12oz (400g) can
tomatoes crushed

12oz (400g) can butter beans

12oz (400g) can kidney beans

12oz (400g) can corn kernels

2 zucchini (courgettes) grated

Add tomatoes, all beans, corn, grated zucchini and heat through.

Step 3 – Finish

2 tablespoons lime juice

garnish: cilantro (fresh coriander)

optional garnish: Cashew & Lime
Aioli or other creamy dressing

Add lime juice and garnish with cilantro and Cashew & Lime Aioli.

Mexican Guacamole Salad

MAKES 8 X 1 CUP SERVES

2 cups baby arugula (rocket)

1½ cups cherry tomatoes halved

½ cup scallions (spring onions) finely sliced (around 1 large)

12oz (400g) can whole kernel corn drained or 2 cups frozen corn

12oz (400g) can black beans drained

1 orange bell pepper (capsicum) finely cubed

GUACAMOLE DRESSING:

1 cup cilantro (fresh coriander)

1 large avocado mashed

2 tablespoons lime juice

2 tablespoons lemon juice

1 tablespoon liquid honey

½ teaspoon salt

½ red onion finely diced

3 tablespoons oil

3 cloves garlic crushed

Add arugula and halved cherry tomatoes to a serving bowl.

Add thinly sliced scallions, corn, black beans and bell pepper.

Put the rest of the salad ingredients into the bowl.

Put the dressing ingredients into a small bowl and mix well. Pour over the salad ingredients and mix through gently.

Soft Corn Tortilla Wedges

SERVES 4

10 soft corn tortillas
1 tablespoon oil or oil spray
garnish: chilli powder

Heat oven to 350°F (180°C).

Cut tortillas into 6 triangles, brush with oil and bake in oven for 12 minutes.

To serve, lightly garnish with chilli powder.

Zingy Tomato Salsa

MACES 3 CUPS

4 large ripe tomatoes

½ small red onion diced finely

¼ cup lime juice

½ teaspoon salt

½ cup cilantro (fresh coriander) chopped

optional: fresh chilli finely chopped

Finely chop the tomatoes and red onion and place in a mixing bowl.

Add lime juice, salt and cilantro and mix well.

Mango & Raspberry Coconut Ice

SERVES 4

....

1 cup coconut milk

2 cups frozen mango

1 cup frozen raspberries

2 tablespoons liquid honey

zest of 1 lemon

garnish: coconut milk/cream

Place ingredients in blender and puree until smooth.

Pour into serving glasses. Garnish with mint and extra coconut milk or cream.

Hold in freezer for up to 10 minutes.

Tip: Take mango and raspberries out of the freezer slightly ahead of time – they should have softened a little but still be frozen.

A Spanish Paella is
so much fun
to make!

Spanish Paella

Creamy Broccoli Salad with Cranberries

Baked Vegetable Chips

Black Almond Fudge

Get ready before you start

Jug	Oven	Counter	Ready on stovetop	Plugged in and ready	Preparation required
Boiling with 1 cup of water	Fan bake 350°F (180°C) Oven tray Baking dish	Chopping board Sharp chefs knife Serving dishes	Large pan	Food processor	Precook 1 cup short grain brown rice

Timing

:00	FUDGE	Make fudge and put into oven.
:06	PAELLA	Start saute up to and including mushrooms and carrots.
:12	CHIPS	Make vege chips and place in oven.
:17	PAELLA	Add rice, tomatoes, green beans, paprika and stock.
:22	SALAD	Toast nuts and seeds and assemble salad ingredients.
:27	PAELLA	Add chickpeas, lime juice and zest, peas and parsley.
:30	FINISH	Serve and enjoy!

Spanish Paella

MAKES 8 X 1 CUP SERVES

Step 1 – Saute Onions

1 onion sliced

2 cloves garlic crushed

1 teaspoon grated ginger

½ green bell pepper (capsicum)

½ red bell pepper (capsicum)

½ red chilli finely chopped

Heat oil in a large pan and saute onion, garlic, ginger, diced bell peppers and chilli for 5 minutes or until soft.

Step 2 – Add Mushrooms & Carrots

1 cup chopped mushrooms

1 carrot julienned

Add mushrooms and carrots and cook for a further 2 minutes.

Step 3 – Add Tomatoes

1 cup short grain brown rice cooked

2 x 12oz (400g) cans tomatoes crushed

4oz (100g) green beans

1 teaspoon smoked paprika

1 ½ cups vegetable stock

Add the rice, tomatoes, green beans, paprika and mix through.

Add the stock, stir until just combined and simmer for 5 minutes or until liquid is absorbed.

Step 4 – Finish & Garnish

12oz (400g) can chickpeas

1 lime, juice and zest

1 cup frozen peas

½ cup chopped parsley

garnish: limes quartered

Add chickpeas, lime juice and zest, peas and parsley and cook for a further 2 minutes.

Place quartered limes on top to serve.

Creamy Broccoli Salad with Cranberries

MAKES 4 X 1 CUP SERVES

¼ cup pumpkin seeds

¼ cup flaked almonds

¼ cup sunflower seeds

2 heads broccoli finely chopped

½ cup cranberries or dried fruit of choice - reserve some for garnish

½ cup chopped parsley

1 cup Cashew & Lemon Aioli

Add nuts and seeds to hot pan and dry roast.

Cut broccoli into small pieces (smaller than bite-size) and add to bowl.

Add nuts and all remaining ingredients.

Cashew & Lemon Aioli

MAKES 1 CUP

1 ½ cups cashew nuts raw

1 clove garlic

2 teaspoons ground coriander

1 tablespoon seeded mustard

4 tablespoons lemon juice (around 2 lemons)

½ cup water

¼ teaspoon salt

optional: 1 teaspoon sweet chilli sauce (or chopped chilli)

Place all ingredients into blender and blend until smooth and creamy.

If needed, add a little more water to achieve the perfect blending consistency.

Baked Vegetable Chips

MABES 4 X 1 CUP SERVES

thinly sliced vegetables:

- 1 medium sweet potato (kumara)
- 2 carrots
- cut bunch of kale leaves
- 1 beetroot sliced thinly
- 1 teaspoon smoked paprika

1 tablespoon oil

1 tablespoon nutritional yeast flakes

1 teaspoon salt

Toss vegetables in oil, smoked paprika, nutritional yeast flakes and salt. You may have to add a little more oil to evenly coat the vegetables.

Bake on an oven tray lined with parchment (baking) paper at 350°F (180°C) for 15 minutes or until cooked.

Serve with aioli or hummus.

Tip: Most root vegetables are suitable for this. For leafy vegetables such as kale, massage a bit of oil and garlic into the leaves.

Tip: Use relatively dry kale or else it will start to steam up.

Tip: Keep an eye on them, if they start to burn give another little spray of oil.

Black Almond Fudge

MAKES 12 PIECES

1 cup dates

1 cup boiling water

½ cup rolled oats

½ cup ground almonds

½ cup carob powder

2 tablespoons liquid honey

12oz (400g) can black beans

1 ripe banana

2 teaspoons vanilla essence

garnish: ½ cup slivered almonds

optional: 1 teaspoon fresh chilli or chilli flakes

Soak the dates in the boiling water for around 5 minutes to soften. Drain.

Put all ingredients (except slivered almonds) into a food processor and blend until a thick lump bounces around the machine.

Add the slivered almonds to the mix but do not blend.

Choose a baking dish around 6x10in (15x25cm). Line with parchment (baking) paper and spoon in the mixture. Flatten out with a spoon.

Bake at 350°F (180°C) for 30 minutes.

Cut into squares using a sharp knife.

Tip: Chilli goes well with chocolate so add some if you like a little heat.

You will love the bursts of flavour in this Sayur Lodeh.

Indonesian Sayur Lodeh Tofu Curry

Rocket, Almond & Fig Salad

Cauliflower Couscous

Peach & Blueberry Crumble

Get ready before you start

Jug	Oven	Counter	Ready on stovetop	Plugged in and ready	Preparation required
Boiling with 4 cups of water	Fan bake 350°F (180°C)	Chopping board	Large pan	Food processor	
	Oven tray	Sharp chefs knife			
		Serving dishes			

Timing

:00	CURRY	Cut pumpkin and place in oven.
:04	CURRY	Saute onion, oil, garlic, ginger, lemongrass.
:07	CRUMBLE	Put fruit in baking dish, add granola on top and place in oven.
:11	CURRY	Add peanut butter, curry paste, salt, honey, water to jug and mix.
:15	COUSCOUS	Blend cauliflower; add oil, turmeric, parsley, mint, lemon juice, salt.
:20	SALAD	Assemble all ingredients.
:25	CURRY	Add beans, tofu, pumpkin, coconut and coconut cream.
:30	FINISH	Serve and enjoy!

Indonesian Sayur Lodeh Tofu Curry

MAKES 10 X 1 CUP SERVES

Step 1 – Roast Pumpkin

2 cups pumpkin chopped ½in (1cm) cubed

spray of oil

Cube the pumpkin and place on oven tray lined with parchment (baking) paper.

Lightly spray the pumpkin with oil and place in oven at 350°F (180°C) for 15-20 minutes or until just soft.

Step 2 – Saute Onion

1 onion sliced finely

1 tablespoon oil

2 large cloves garlic crushed

2 tablespoons ginger puree

2 tablespoons (about 1 stick) lemongrass (fresh or frozen) finely chopped

In a large pan saute onion, oil, garlic, ginger, lemongrass.

Step 3 – Make Peanut Paste

¾ cup peanut butter

4 cups boiling water

2 teaspoons Thai red curry paste

½ teaspoon salt

2 tablespoons liquid honey

Add peanut butter, boiling water, curry paste, salt and honey to large pouring jug and stir until ingredients are mixed together, then add to pan.

Step 4 – Finish

3 cups white cabbage finely sliced

2 cups green beans fresh or frozen

14oz (400g) pack firm tofu

3 tablespoons shredded coconut

7oz (200ml) coconut cream

garnish: 2 tablespoons finely chopped roasted peanuts

garnish: ¼ cup cilantro (fresh coriander)

Add sliced cabbage, green beans and tofu and cook for 2 minutes. Add coconut and coconut cream.

Garnish with chopped peanuts and cilantro.

Rocket, Almond & Fig Salad

MAKES 3 X 1 CUP SERVES

3 cups arugula (rocket) or baby spinach

¼ cup flaked almonds

1 cup figs fresh or dried open and cut in half

¼ cup walnuts

1 tablespoon lemon juice (around ½ a lemon)

Put arugula in shallow serving dish and add all other ingredients on top.

Tip: Rinse arugula in water to freshen up.

Cauliflower Couscous

MAKES 3 X 1 CUP SERVES

1 small cauliflower

½ cup chopped mint

½ cup chopped parsley

1 tablespoon lemon juice

¼ tablespoon salt

¼ teaspoon oil

½ teaspoon turmeric

Cut cauliflower into small pieces and add to food processor.

Blend until you have a rice-like texture.

Do not overprocess or it will go mushy.

Add remaining ingredients.

Serve as couscous.

Peach & Blueberry Crumble

MAKES 8 X 1 CUP SERVES

2 x 12oz (400g) cans peaches drained

2 cups frozen blueberries

12oz (400g) can apple sauce

3 cups granola (muesli)

oil spray

garnish: cashew cream

Drain peaches and add to baking dish. Layer blueberries on top and add apple sauce.

Pour granola over top and spray lightly with oil.

Bake at 350°F (180°C) for 25 minutes or until golden brown.

Serve with cashew cream.

These are lovely, fresh and flavoursome Asian dishes.

Fresh Rice Paper Rolls

Asian Dipping Sauce

Gado Gado

Sweet Berry Iced Tea

Get ready before you start

Jug	Oven	Counter	Ready on stovetop	Plugged in and ready	Preparation required
Boiling with 7 cups of water		Chopping board Sharp chefs knife Serving dishes and glasses	Medium frying pan Medium pot	Blender or stick blender	

Timing

:00	GADO	Put potatoes on to boil for 15 minutes or until tender.
:03	GADO	Saute tofu, oil, salt.
:07	SAUCE	Add all ingredients to blender and blend until smooth.
:10	GADO	Prepare vegetables and add in colour clumps to serving bowl.
:14	ROLLS	Prepare vegetables.
:17	DRINK	Pour boiling water over tea bags.
:18	GADO	Put beans in potatoes.
:19	ROLLS	Add a little of each of the prepared ingredients and make rolls.
:24	GADO	Add beans, potatoes and tofu to bowl of vegetables.
:27	DRINK	Finish tea.
:30	FINISH	Serve and enjoy!

Fresh Rice Paper Rolls

MAKES 16 ½ ROLLS

8 rice paper wrappers

4oz(100g) vermicelli noodles

¼ cup cilantro (fresh coriander), mint or basil chopped

1 cup thinly sliced savoy cabbage

1 cucumber thinly julienned

2 avocados thinly sliced

1 red bell pepper (capsicum) thinly julienned

1 carrot thinly julienned

While noodles are still in the package, use your hand to press down and break them up a bit. Soak in boiling water until soft then drain.

Take a sheet of rice paper and soak in a shallow bowl of hot water until it is soft – about 20 seconds.

Place rice paper sheet onto a plate and top with vermicelli, herbs, fresh vegetables and peanuts below the halfway mark of the round, leaving an edge. Fold in both sides, securely fold the bottom edge over the filling to enclose, and then carefully roll to the end.

Cut in half and serve with Asian dipping sauce.

Asian Dipping Sauce

MAKES ¼ CUP

1 small chilli finely diced

2 tablespoons liquid honey

2 tablespoons soy sauce or tamari

2 tablespoons lime juice (around 1 lime)

1 tablespoon sesame oil

Add all ingredients to a small bowl and stir until well combined.

Gado Gado

MAKES 8 X 1 CUP SERVES

2 cups potatoes chopped into ½in (1cm) cubes

⅛ teaspoon salt (for potatoes)

1 teaspoon oil (for potatoes)

10oz (300g) firm tofu cubed

2 teaspoons oil

½ teaspoon salt

1 cup green beans

1 cup red cherry tomatoes halved

1 cup yellow cherry tomatoes halved

1 cup cucumber diced

1 cup red cabbage thinly sliced

garnish: cilantro (fresh coriander)

Put the potatoes into a pot with boiling water and cook for 15 minutes or until they are soft. Drain.

In a pot or pan saute the tofu, oil and salt for around 10 minutes or until the tofu is browned.

Lightly steam green beans. Slice all other vegetables and place in sections in main serving dish.

Sprinkle salt and drizzle olive oil over warm potatoes and add to bowl.

Add the warm tofu and drizzle sauce over the top. Garnish with freshly chopped cilantro. Mix just before you serve.

Tip: You can serve on the table in one big dish like the photo, or you can portion out into individual bowls so everyone can mix their own plate.

Tip: This dish relies on the tofu and potato being hot. You may like to heat the sauce in a pot before serving if all the ingredients are cold.

Gado Gado Sauce

MAKES 1 CUP

1 cup roasted peanuts (or ¾ cup peanut butter)

2 tablespoons lime juice (around 1 lime)

1 tablespoon liquid honey

1 tablespoon sesame oil

1 tablespoon soy sauce or tamari

1 tablespoon ginger puree

2 cloves garlic

¼ cup water

optional: 1 teaspoon tamarind paste

Put the sauce ingredients into a blender and blend until you have a smooth sauce.

Add more water if needed to achieve smooth blending.

Sweet Berry Iced Tea

MAKES 5 CUPS

8 berry herbal tea bags

1 ½ cups hot water

1 ½ cups ice

1 cup cold water

1 cup fruit juice (pomegranate, cranberry or any juice of choice)

garnish: blueberries and mint leaves

Add tea bags to hot water and leave covered for 10 minutes.

Add ice, cold water and fruit juice to serving jug.

Remove tea bags from hot water and add tea to jug.

Garnish with blueberries and mint leaves.

This is the ultimate breakfast to start your day. Plus make this delicious stir fry to take for your lunch!

**Five Grain
Hot Breakfast**

**Super Quick
Thai Vegetable
Stir Fry**

Get ready before you start

Jug	Oven	Counter	Ready on stovetop	Plugged in and ready	Preparation required
Boiling with 4 cups of water		Chopping board Sharp chefs knife Serving dishes	Large pan Medium pot	Blender or stick blender	

Timing

:00	GRAINS	Put grains on stove to simmer.
:03	STIR FRY	Saute onion, garlic, ginger, oil.
:08	STIR FRY	Add chopped carrots, red bell pepper, zucchini, mushrooms.
:15	HUMMUS	Add all ingredients to blender and blend until smooth.
:20	STIR FRY	Add asparagus, red cabbage, salt, tamari.
:26	GRAINS	Add grain to bowl and add milk, flax seed oil, fruit, nuts, seeds.
:30	FINISH	Serve and enjoy!

Five Grain Hot Breakfast

I have a breakfast like this most mornings and it is a great start to the day.
MAKES 2 X 1 CUP SERVES

1 cup Five Grain Cereal cooked

1/8 cup milk such as hemp, almond, rice, soy, cashew

1 teaspoon flax seed oil

1 cup fresh fruit such as bananas, pears, apples, blueberries, raspberries, boysenberries

1/8 cup nuts such as pecans, almonds, walnuts

1/8 cup seeds such as sunflower, pumpkin, sesame

Put hot cooked mixed grains into cereal bowl. Add a little milk and a touch of flax seed oil.

Add fruit, nuts and seeds.

Five Grain Cereal

SERVES 4

MAKE IN ADVANCE IN BULK:

1 cup brown rice

1 cup millet hulled

1 cup amaranth

1 cup white quinoa

1 cup buckwheat

1 cup red quinoa

TO COOK 4 SERVES:

1 cup of mixed grains

a touch of salt

4 cups boiling water

Put all ingredients into a pot and heat until boiling.

Turn down to a low heat and let it simmer for 25–30 minutes. Put the lid on. Do not stir.

Tip: You can also cook this in a slow cooker. It takes approximately 1 hour on high.

Super Quick Thai Vegetable Stir Fry

MAKES 10 X 1 CUP SERVES

Step 1 – Saute Onion

1 onion chopped

1 teaspoon oil

1 clove garlic crushed

1 teaspoon ginger puree

1 tablespoon Thai curry paste

In a large pan saute onion, oil, garlic, ginger and Thai curry paste for 5 minutes or until onion is just soft.

Step 2 – Saute Vegetables

1 carrot chopped into diagonal half moons

1 red bell pepper (capsicum) cubed

3 stalks celery

1 zucchini (courgette)

6 button mushrooms

Add carrot, bell pepper, celery, zucchini, mushrooms and cook for 5 minutes.

Step 3 – Saute Remaining Veges

10 stalks asparagus

¼ red cabbage

Break woody ends off asparagus and add the tops to the pan. Add red cabbage. Cook for 2 minutes.

Step 4 – Finish

12oz (400g) can red beans

½ teaspoon salt

1 teaspoon tamari (or soy sauce)

2 tablespoons lime juice (around 1 lime)

2 cups cooked brown rice

optional: hummus to serve

Add red beans, salt, tamari, lime juice and rice and warm through.

Episode 47

These aromatic and flavoursome dishes make a lovely combination.

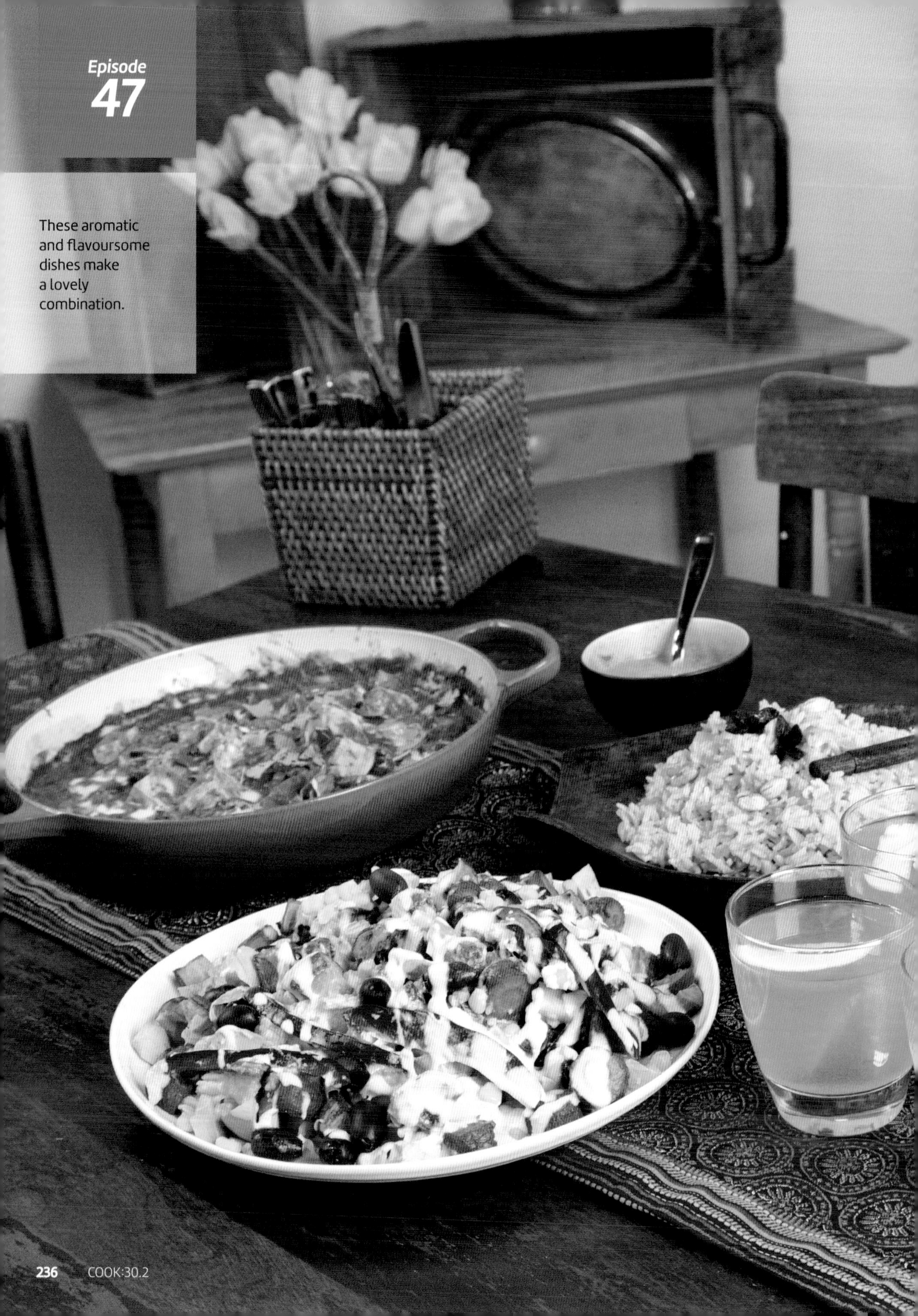

Aromatic Cambodian Tofu Curry

Root Vegetable & Cos Salad

Orange Dressing

Cinnamon & Cardamom Rice

Lemon Ginger Honey Soother

Get ready before you start

Jug	Oven	Counter	Ready on stovetop	Plugged in and ready	Preparation required
Boiling with 6 cups of water	Fan bake 350°F (180°C) Oven tray	Chopping board Sharp chefs knife Serving dishes and glasses	Large pan Medium pot		

Timing

:00	RICE	Start to saute onion and oil.
:02	SALAD	Put sweet potato and carrots on to roast.
:04	RICE	Add rice, cinnamon, cardamom, star anise and sauted onion to pot.
:06	CURRY	Saute onion, garlic, lemongrass.
:11	CURRY	Add all remaining ingredients.
:16	SALAD	Add all ingredients to serving dish, layer by layer.
:22	DRESSING	Make orange dressing.
:25	SOOTHER	Assemble ingredients and pour into glasses.
:29	RICE	Remove spice pods from rice and serve.
:30	FINISH	Serve and enjoy!

Aromatic Cambodian Tofu Curry

MAKES 8 X 1 CUP SERVES

Step 1 – Saute Onion

1½ cups diced onion

2 cloves garlic crushed

2 tablespoons lemongrass chopped

1 large red bell pepper (capsicum) largely diced

1 tablespoon ginger puree

1 tablespoon chilli paste (optional)

½ cup cilantro (fresh coriander) stalks

1 tablespoon fennel seeds

1 tablespoon oil

Saute onion, garlic, lemongrass, bell pepper, ginger, chilli paste, cilantro stems, fennel seeds and oil for 5 minutes or until onion is just soft.

Step 2 – Add Spices, Tomatoes, Beans

½ teaspoon clove powder

½ teaspoon turmeric powder

12oz (400g) can crushed tomatoes

2 tablespoons liquid honey

½ teaspoon salt

1 cup long green beans halved

Add clove powder and turmeric and stir through briefly before adding the tomatoes, honey, salt and long green beans.

Step 3 – Finish

12oz (400g) firm tofu cubed into large chunks

12oz (400ml) can coconut milk

garnish: cilantro (fresh coriander)

Add tofu and coconut milk, stirring gently so you do not damage the tofu.

Turn pan down to a very low heat. You don't want it bubbling as this will change the consistency of the dish.

Serve with a garnish of cilantro.

Root Vegetable & Cos Salad

MAKES 8 X 1 CUP SERVES

2 cups orange sweet potato (kumara) diced ½in (1cm)

2 cups carrots diced ½in (1cm)

1 teaspoon oil

4 cups cos lettuce thinly sliced

1 cup sliced red bell pepper (capsicum)

½ x 12oz (400g) can whole kernel corn drained (around 1 cup)

1 avocado diced

20 kalamata olives (pitted)

Mix the sweet potato and carrots with the oil and put on an oven tray. Bake at 350°F (180°C) for around 20 minutes or until soft.

Slice the cos lettuce and add to serving bowl. Add bell pepper, corn, avocado, olives and the roasted sweet potato and carrots.

Optional: Drizzle over a cashew aioli or a coconut yoghurt dressing.

Orange Dressing

This is a nice spoonover for a curry.
MAKES 1 CUP

4 tablespoons orange juice (around 1 orange)

¼ cup tahini

1 tablespoon maple syrup

½ teaspoon salt

Add orange juice and tahini to a small bowl and stir until well combined.

Add maple syrup and salt and mix well.

Cinnamon & Cardamom Rice

MAKES 3 CUPS

1½ cups diced onion (around 1 onion)

1 teaspoon oil

1 cup basmati rice

2 cups boiling water

½ teaspoon salt

2 cinnamon sticks

6 cardamom pods

2 star anise pods

In a medium pot saute onion and oil.

Add cinnamon sticks, cardamom pods and star anise.

Add rice, water and salt to pot and simmer on a low heat for 25 minutes with the lid on.

Lemon Ginger Honey Soother

SERVES 4

1 sprig of fresh ginger unpeeled (about the size of your thumb)

2 tablespoons liquid honey

2 tablespoons lemon juice (around 1 lemon)

4 lemon slices

boiling water

Slice ginger into thin strips and put into a glass with honey, lemon juice, and lemon slices.

Pour boiling water over it and stir.

Stand for several minutes to let the flavours mingle.

Stir again and serve with the ginger and lemon slices in the cup or glass.

This slaw is so fresh and tasty, and a nice accompaniment to this hearty meal.

French Lentil Ragout

Polenta & Cherry Tomato Mingle

Potato & Butternut Mash

Apple & Fennel Slaw

Grape Juice Cocktail

Get ready before you start

Jug	Oven	Counter	Ready on stovetop	Plugged in and ready	Preparation required
Boiling with 7 cups of water		Chopping board Sharp chefs knife Serving dishes	Large pan Medium pot Small frying pan	Food processor	

Timing

:00	MASH	Put potatoes and pumpkin on to boil.
:04	RAGOUT	Saute soft vegetables and add mixed herbs.
:08	SLAW	Grate fresh ingredients and assemble salad on serving dish.
:11	POLENTA	Saute polenta cubes.
:14	RAGOUT	Make sauce, add lentils.
:17	MASH	Drain potatoes, pumpkin, add milk, salt, parsley and mash roughly.
:20	POLENTA	Add asparagus to saute pan. Finish dish with cherry tomatoes.
:23	COCKTAIL	Add grape, pomegranate juice, soda water, ice and mint to jug.
:30	FINISH	Serve and enjoy!

French Lentil Ragout

MAKES 5 X 1 CUP SERVES

Step 1 – Saute Vegetables

1 tablespoon oil

1½ cups onion finely diced (around 1 onion)

3 cloves garlic crushed

2 cups aubergine (eggplant) diced (around 1 large)

15 button mushrooms cut in half

2 cups zucchini (courgettes) chopped (around 2 medium)

1 red bell pepper (capsicum)

1 teaspoon mixed herbs

In a pot or pan saute the oil, onion, garlic, aubergine, mushrooms, zucchini, bell pepper and mixed herbs for 8 minutes or until soft.

Step 2 – Mix Sauce

2 tablespoons soy sauce

½ teaspoon salt

1 teaspoon liquid honey

2 teaspoons arrowroot (or 3 teaspoons cornstarch/cornflour)

1 cup cold water

In a cup mix the soy sauce, salt, honey, arrowroot and cold water. Pour into the ragout and stir until it is well mixed.

Step 3 – Add Lentils

2 x 12oz (400g) cans brown lentils

Add the lentils.

You may need to add some more water, or cook for a little longer to achieve the correct consistency.

Step 4 – Serve

garnish: cilantro (fresh coriander)

Garnish with cilantro.

Polenta & Cherry Tomato Mingle

MAKES 3 X 1 CUP SERVES

18oz (510g) block of precooked store bought polenta cut into cubes

2 teaspoons oil

½ teaspoon salt

½ cup yellow cherry tomatoes

½ cup red cherry tomatoes

10 stalks asparagus

Cut cubes of polenta and add to a hot pan with oil, sprinkle with salt and fry lightly.

Break woody ends off the asparagus and discard. Cut remainder of asparagus stalks in half.

Add asparagus stalks to pan and fry lightly until polenta is starting to crisp on the edges but asparagus is still firm to the bite.

Add cherry tomatoes to bowl, add the polenta and asparagus and mix together.

Tip: Alternatively you can make your own polenta by mixing polenta and boiling water and letting sit for 10-20 minutes to set (or follow packet directions).

Potato & Butternut Mash

MAKES 5 X 1 CUP SERVES

2 large washed potatoes roughly cubed

2 cups pumpkin peeled and cubed

7 cups boiling water

½ cup milk of your choice

¾ teaspoon salt

2 tablespoons parsley chopped

Add potatoes, pumpkin and water to medium pot and bring to boil.

Cook for 15 minutes or until soft.

Drain and mash with milk, salt and parsley.

Apple & Fennel Slaw

MAKES 6 X 1 CUP SERVES

½ white cabbage sliced finely

1 fennel sliced finely

2 carrots grated

1 apple grated

2 cups baby spinach

½ cup mint

1 tablespoon maple syrup

¼ cup freshly squeezed orange juice (around 1 orange)

1 tablespoon olive oil

½ teaspoon salt

Using your food processor and it's slicing and grating attachments, chop cabbage, fennel, carrot and apple (with core cut out). Add to serving dish with baby spinach and chopped mint.

Drizzle maple syrup, orange juice, olive oil and salt over top.

Tip: If you don't have a food processor just use a sharp knife and hand grater to slice vegetables thinly.

Grape Juice Cocktail

MAKES 4 X 1 CUP SERVES

1 cup ice

1½ cups grape juice

½ cup pomegranate juice

1 cup soda water

handful of fresh mint leaves

Add ice to serving jug followed by grape juice, pomegranate juice, soda water and mint.

This creamy risotto will surprise you – even more so when you add the Parmeshew Cheese!

**Beetroot &
Fennel Risotto**

**Garlicky
Cilantro
Chickpeas**

**Parmeshew
Cheese**

**Mediterranean
Vegetable
Mingle**

**Strawberry
Cheesecake
Glasses**

Get ready before you start

Jug	Oven	Counter	Ready on stovetop	Plugged in and ready	Preparation required
		Chopping board	Large frying pan	Blender or stick blender	Precook short grain brown rice, beetroot and chickpeas
		Sharp chefs knife	Large pot	Food processor	
		Serving dishes and glasses	Small fry pan panpan		

Timing

:00	RISOTTO	Saute onion, celery, garlic, fennel seeds and oil.
:04	CHEESE	Blend cashews and yeast flakes until fine.
:06	RISOTTO	Add rice, beetroot and stock.
:09	DESSERT	Add ingredients to food processor, finish glasses and put in freezer.
:20	VEGES	Saute vegetables.
:26	CHICKPEAS	Saute chickpeas, oil, salt and garlic.
:30	FINISH	Serve and enjoy!

Beetroot & Fennel Risotto

MAKES 6 X 1 CUP SERVES

....

Step 1 – Saute Onion & Celery

1 onion diced
2 stalks celery sliced
1 clove garlic crushed
1 tablespoon fennel seeds
½ teaspoon oil

Saute onion, celery, garlic, fennel seeds and oil for 5 minutes or until onion is soft.

....

Step 2 – Rice & Beetroot

3 cups cooked short grain rice
2 precooked beetroot grated
4 cups vegetable stock

Add rice and stir.

Add beetroot and stock. Keep cooking until liquid is all absorbed.

....

Step 3 – Finish

½ cup pumpkin seeds
¼ cup chopped parsley
4 tablespoons Parmeshew Cheese
garnish: Italian parsley

Add pumpkin seeds and Parmeshew Cheese which will add creaminess to the risotto as well as a nice flavour.

Garnish with Italian parsley, extra pumpkin seeds and a sprinkle of Parmeshew Cheese.

....

Garlicky Cilantro Chickpeas

The simplicity of this dish makes it very tasty.
MAKES 3 X 1 CUP SERVES

12oz can (400g) chickpeas
(garbanzo beans)

2 teaspoons oil

½ teaspoon salt

2 cloves garlic crushed

garnish: ¼ cup cilantro
(fresh coriander)

Add chickpeas to hot pan with oil, salt and garlic and saute lightly for
2 minutes.

Garnish with cilantro.

Parmeshew Cheese

A great alternative to Parmesan Cheese.
MAKES 1 CUP

1 cup cashew nuts raw

2 tablespoons nutritional yeast flakes

Put ingredients into a blender and blend for
30 seconds or until you get a bread crumb texture.
The time will depend on your blender.

You may have to use a spoon to take the mixture
off the sides of the blender and re-blend to get
it consistent.

Tip: This will store in your fridge for weeks. Keep some
on hand to spice up your food!

Mediterranean Vegetable Mingle

Colour is the most important ingredient in this dish!
MAKES 4 X 1 CUP SERVES

1 tablespoon oil

4 cloves garlic crushed

1 cup red onion thickly diced
(around 1 onion)

1 cup red bell pepper (capsicum)
thickly diced (around 1 capsicum)

1 cup yellow bell pepper (capsicum)
thickly diced (around 1 capsicum)

1 cup orange bell pepper
(capsicum) thickly diced (around
1 capsicum)

1 cup zucchini (courgette) thickly
diced (around 1 large)

10 stalks asparagus cut into 1in
(2cm) pieces

1 teaspoon salt

1 cup black olives

garnish: parsley

In a pan saute the oil, garlic and onion for 5 minutes or until soft.

Add the other vegetables and saute for 5 more minutes or until they are soft but still firm.

Sprinkle with salt, add the olives and stir.

Strawberry Cheesecake Glasses

SERVES 4

BASE:

1 cup almonds

¾ cup dates

¼ cup desiccated coconut

TOPPING

1½ cups cashew nuts raw

4 tablespoons lime juice

¼ cup coconut oil melted

¾ cup water

3 tablespoons liquid honey

1 cup frozen strawberries

garnish: blueberries

garnish: mint

Place almonds, dates and coconut into food processor and blend until a fine texture. Press into serving glasses to create the base.

In a blender add cashews, lime juice, coconut oil, water and honey and blend until mixture is smooth and creamy.

Add strawberries and blend well, scraping down the sides of the blender as needed.

Pour mixture onto the base and spread evenly.

Place in freezer to set.

Can be stored in the fridge once set.

Roasted
cauliflower tastes
amazing and
makes a wonderful
salad.

Vietnamese Pho Noodles

Fresh Buckwheat Tabouli

Indian Spiced Roasted Cauliflower Salad

Warm Cashew Carob Chai

Get ready before you start

Jug	Oven	Counter	Ready on stovetop	Plugged in and ready	Preparation required
Boiling with 12 cups of water	Fan bake 350°F (180°C)	Chopping board	Large pan	Blender	
	Oven tray	Sharp chefs knife	Large pot		
		Serving dishes and glasses	Medium frying pan		

Timing

:00	CAULI	Prepare cauliflower mix and place in oven.
:06	PHO	Saute onion, oil, garlic, ginger, bell pepper, carrot.
:09	TABOULI	Put buckwheat and water on to boil.
:10	PHO	Put noodles in hot water and fry tofu slabs with a little oil.
:15	PHO	Add cinnamon, coriander, boiling water and soy sauce.
:17	AIOLI/CAULI	Make aioli and drizzle over served cauliflower. Add baby spinach.
:20	TABOULI	Finish tabouli with cucumber, cherry tomatoes.
:23	PHO	Add honey, noodles, tofu to main pan.
:24	CHAI	Blend all ingredients together and serve.
:30	FINISH	Serve and enjoy!

Vietnamese Pho Noodles

MAKES 6 X 1 CUP SERVES

....

Step 1 – Saute Vegetables

1 cup onion sliced thinly (around 1 medium onion)

1 tablespoon oil

2 tablespoons ginger puree

1 carrot sliced into half moons

1 red bell pepper (capsicum) thickly diced

Saute onion, oil, ginger, carrot and bell pepper for 5 minutes or until soft.

....

Step 2 – Prepare Noodles & Tofu

3oz (100g) thin rice noodles (vermicelli)

boiling water to cover

10oz (300g) firm tofu

1 tablespoon oil

Break noodles and place in a bowl. Cover noodles with boiling water and leave for 10 minutes or until soft.

Slice tofu into slabs approximately 1x3x½in (2x6x1cm) and fry lightly in a small pan each side until golden.

....

Step 3 – Add Flavour & Simmer

¼ teaspoon cinnamon

1 teaspoon ground coriander

4 cups boiling water

2 tablespoons soy sauce

Into the main pan add cinnamon, coriander, boiling water, soy sauce and simmer for 15 minutes.

If the dish dries out you may have to add more water.

When cooked stir in the drained noodles and cooked tofu.

....

Step 4 – Toppings

cilantro (fresh coriander) roughly chopped

lime wedges

scallions (spring onions) sliced diagonally

Serve the soup in a bowl and add liberal amounts of the topping ingredients, clustering them in different corners of the bowl.

....

Fresh Buckwheat Tabouli

MAKES 6 X 1 CUP SERVES

1 cup buckwheat raw

2 cups boiling water

8 sundried tomatoes sliced

½ cup red cherry tomatoes halved

½ cup yellow cherry tomatoes halved

½ red onion finely diced

1½ cups cucumber finely diced

1½ cups parsley finely chopped

2 tablespoons lemon juice (around 1 lemon)

1 tablespoon olive oil

Add buckwheat and boiling water to medium pot and cook with the lid on for 10 minutes or until soft.

Add all remaining ingredients to bowl and mix together with your hands.

Tip: 2 cups boiling water with 1 cup raw buckwheat makes 3 cups of cooked buckwheat.

Indian Spiced Roasted Cauliflower Salad

MAKES 6 X 1 CUP SERVES

1 cup onion sliced thinly (around 1 medium onion)

1 teaspoon oil

1 cauliflower

1 tablespoon curry powder

1 tablespoon garam masala

1 tablespoon mustard seeds

2 teaspoons turmeric

¾ cup Cashew & Lime Aioli

2 cups baby spinach

Saute onion and oil for 5 minutes or until soft.

Cut cauliflower florets into bite-sized pieces. Place on oven tray lined with parchment (baking) paper.

Into the onion pan add curry powder, garam masala, mustard seeds and turmeric and stir for about 30 seconds.

Add to cauliflower and toss gently to coat cauliflower with spice mix.

You may lightly spray with oil to prevent from burning. Bake at 350°F (180°C) for 20 minutes or until just soft.

Take out of oven and mix gently together with Cashew & Lime Aioli and baby spinach.

Garnish with extra aioli.

Cashew & Lime Aioli

MAKES 1 CUP

1½ cups cashew nuts raw

1 clove garlic

2 teaspoons ground coriander

1 tablespoon seeded mustard

4 tablespoons lime juice (around 2 limes)

½ cup water

¼ teaspoon salt

optional: 1 teaspoon sweet chilli sauce or chilli paste

Place all ingredients into blender and blend until smooth and creamy.

Add more water if needed to achieve smooth blending consistency.

Warm Cashew Carob Chai

SERVES 4

1 cup cashew nuts raw
¼ teaspoon vanilla essence
2 tablespoons liquid honey
1 tablespoon coconut shredded
1 tablespoon carob powder
1 teaspoon ginger puree
$1/8$ teaspoon cinnamon
$1/8$ teaspoon clove powder
3 cups boiling water

Place ingredients and ½ cup of the boiling water into blender and blend well until creamy. Add remaining water and blend until mixed.

Serve warm.

Tip: To make as a cold drink, use cold water instead of boiling water and add ice cubes.

Three Angels Broadcasting Network

What is 3ABN?

Three Angels Broadcasting Network is an international media group that broadcasts positive Christian lifestyle programming. Their wide variety of health, family, and biblical topics are designed to appeal to a multicultural audience.

3ABN Programming Offers

- Health Topics
- Cooking
- Addiction Help
- Parenting Tips
- Children's Programs
- Music

- Testimonies
- Bible Prophecy
- Inspired Preaching
- Mission Reports
- LIVE Events
- . . . Free Offers and More!

Lighting the world with the glory of God's truth!

LIVE streaming online at 3ABN.tv

  | tv | radio | music | books

WATCH 3ABN
on your mobile device
3ABN app for Android™ and iPhone/iPad

For a complete listing of networks and ways to watch, visit 3ABN.org.
For more information about our ministry or available materials,
call us at (618) 627-4651 (international calls, dial +1 618 627-4651)

Index